THE Student's Cookbook

Ingredients • Techniques • Recipes

Publisher's Note: Raw or semi-cooked eggs should not be consumed by babies, toddlers, pregnant or breastfeeding women, the elderly or those suffering from a chronic illness.

Publisher & Creative Director: Nick Wells
Senior Project Editor: Catherine Taylor
Editorial: Esme Chapman
Art Director: Mike Spender
Layout Design: Jane Ashley
Digital Design & Production: Chris Herbert

Special thanks to Laura Bulbeck and Frances Bodiam.

This is a **FLAME TREE** Book

FLAME TREE PUBLISHING
Crabtree Hall, Crabtree Lane
Fulham, London SW6 6TY
United Kingdom
www.flametreepublishing.com

First published 2014

A copy of the CIP data for this book is available from the British Library.

Printed in Singapore

All images © Flame Tree Publishing Ltd, except for the following images, which are courtesy Shutterstock.com and the following contributors: mangostock 6; CandyBox Images 7; Elena Elisseeva 13; Mert Toker 14; Elen 15; Somchai Som 16; ifong 17; Gayvoronskaya_Yana 18; Joe Belanger 19; Jacek Chabraszewski 20; philippou 21; Olga Drabovich 22; Steve Cukrov 23; Mirabelle Pictures 24; Designsstock 25; Julian Rovagnati 26; ventdusud 27; Nicholas Rjabow 30; M. Unal Ozmen 31; Natalila Pyzhova 32; O. Bellini 33; bitt24 34; Sea Wave 34; Anthony Berenyi 35; Kovaleva_Ka 36; marco mayer 37; Robyn Mackenzie 38; siamionau pavel 39; Allen W Yoo 40; Brent Hofacker 41; cenap refik ongan 41; Péter Gudella 42; fredredhat 43; James Peragine 44; travellight 45; Photoseeker 47; Steven Collins 48; Douglas Freer 49; Medwether 50; Brett Mulcahy 51; Monika Wisniewska 52; Sakuoka 52; bogumil 53; HLPhoto 55; D7INAMI7S 56; Joerg Beuge 57; Olga Miltsova 57; hrk422 58; Louella938 59; kp2107 60; travellight 61; Viktor1 28, 29, 54; Joe Gough 46, 49.

THE Student's Cookbook

Ingredients • Techniques • Recipes

FLAME TREE PUBLISHING

Contents

Essentials 8

Soups & Small Meals 62

Easy-peasy Pasta & Noodles 112

Curries & Rice Dishes 142

Hearty Meals 180

Impress Your Friends 210

Treats & Desserts 230

Index 254

Introduction

ℰ

Most students go off to university feeling confident, grown up and completely sure of their own ability to look after themselves. Of course, then they get there and realise that not only do they have to make new friends, find their way around a new place and study what is possibly a new subject at a much higher level, but Mum and Dad aren't there to do the washing and make the dinner. This book won't remind you to put your washing on, or stop you from putting that one red sock in making all of your whites pink, but it will help make the daunting prospect of cooking simple and possibly even enjoyable.

Money, Money, Money

First things first: food is expensive. That's just one of those sad facts of life we all have to get used to...but that doesn't mean you have to live off baked beans for the next three years. You can if you want to but it's unlikely you would have picked up this book if you intended to do that. It's possible to eat decent food while staying within your student budget and leaving enough money to go out for drinks. It's all about what you cook, how you cook it and how you store it. The recipes you'll find in here give guidelines for how to get the most out of what freezer space you have, show you how to cook anything from a boiled egg to risotto (actually risotto is easy, but looks really impressive if you cook it for a date, or friends), all within a budget. Some recipes can be made a bit fancier if you're cooking right after you get your loan, or cheaper if it's those last few weeks before the next instalment.

Get Kitted Out and Stock Up

It would be useful before you do your first food shop (don't worry if it's too late, you can nip to the local supermarket and pick up anything you need) to have a read through the first part of this book. That will let you know what you're likely to need and what's useful to have in your cupboard for those days you overran at the library, or had every intention of going to the library and went to the pub, and you don't have long before you go out. Don't forget about equipment either – you don't need anything fancy, but there are some things that are worth spending a few quid on that will come in handy again and again.

The Basics

You'll also see useful information such as how to cook eggs or potatoes and a quick guide to what all those cooking words mean. If you already know all of that, then great, smile smugly to yourself and only refer to that bit if you forget. Everyone else, have a good look and save yourself the embarrassment of needing to call home every night to ask.

Get Cooking

The recipes themselves are pretty easy to do, and lots of them will do more than one meal so you won't waste all the food that only comes in packs of twos or more. Even the more complicated-looking recipes are easier than you think. Eating food you have made instead of takeaway every night saves you a fortune and helps stave off the dreaded Freshers' Flu, not to mention makes you feel pretty good about yourself. So ditch the beans and the pizza menu, grab that wooden spoon and have a go.

Introduction

Essentials

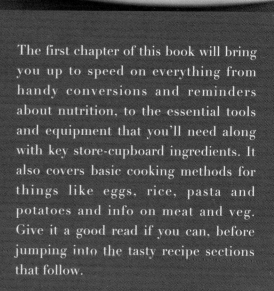

The first chapter of this book will bring you up to speed on everything from handy conversions and reminders about nutrition, to the essential tools and equipment that you'll need along with key store-cupboard ingredients. It also covers basic cooking methods for things like eggs, rice, pasta and potatoes and info on meat and veg. Give it a good read if you can, before jumping into the tasty recipe sections that follow.

Useful Conversions

Oven Temperatures

110°C	225°F	Gas Mark $1/4$	Very slow oven
120/130°C	250°F	Gas Mark $1/2$	Very slow oven
140°C	275°F	Gas Mark 1	Slow oven
150°C	300°F	Gas Mark 2	Slow oven
160/170°C	325°F	Gas Mark 3	Moderate oven
180°C	350°F	Gas Mark 4	Moderate oven
190°C	375°F	Gas Mark 5	Moderately hot
200°C	400°F	Gas Mark 6	Moderately hot
220°C	425°F	Gas Mark 7	Hot oven
230°C	450°F	Gas Mark 8	Hot oven
240°C	475°F	Gas Mark 9	Very hot oven

Dry Weights

Metric	Imperial	Metric	Imperial
10 g	$1/4$ oz	175 g	6 oz
15 g	$1/2$ oz	185 g	$6^{1/2}$ oz
20 g	$3/4$ oz	200 g	7 oz
25 g	1 oz	225 g	8 oz
40 g	$1^{1/2}$ oz	250 g	9 oz
50 g	2 oz	275 g	10 oz
65 g	$2^{1/2}$ oz	300 g	11 oz
75 g	3 oz	325 g	$11^{1/2}$ oz
100 g	$3^{1/2}$ oz	350 g	12 oz
125 g	4 oz	375 g	13 oz
130 g	$4^{1/2}$ oz	400 g	14 oz
150 g	5 oz	425 g	15 oz
165 g	$5^{1/2}$ oz	450 g	1 lb (16 oz)

Liquid Measures

Metric	Imperial
2.5 ml	$1/2$ teaspoon
5 ml	1 teaspoon
15 ml	1 tablespoon
25 ml	1 fl oz
50 ml	2 fl oz
65 ml	$2^{1}/2$ fl oz
85 ml	3 fl oz
100 ml	$3^{1}/2$ fl oz
125 ml	4 fl oz
135 ml	$4^{1}/2$ fl oz
150 ml	$1/4$ pint (5 fl oz)
175 ml	6 fl oz
200 ml	7 fl oz ($1/3$ pint)
250 ml	8 fl oz
275 ml	9 fl oz
300 ml	$1/2$ pint (10 fl oz)
350 ml	12 fl oz
400 ml	14 fl oz
450 ml	$3/4$ pint (15 fl oz)
475 ml	16 fl oz
500 ml	18 fl oz
600 ml	1 pint (20 fl oz)
750 ml	$1^{1}/4$ pints
900 ml	$1^{1}/2$ pints
1 litre	$1^{3}/4$ pints
1.1 litres	2 pints
1.25 litres	$2^{1}/4$ pints
1.5 litres	$2^{1}/2$ pints
1.6 litres	$2^{3}/4$ pints
1.7 litres	3 pints
2 litres	$3^{1}/2$ pints
2.25 litres	4 pints
2.5 litres	$4^{1}/2$ pints
2.75 litres	5 pints

Temperature Conversions

°F	°C	°F	°C
−4°F	−20°C	68°F	20°C
5°F	−15°C	77°F	25°C
14°F	−10°C	86°F	30°C
23°F	−5°C	95°F	35°C
32°F	0°C	104°F	40°C
41°F	5°C	113°F	45°C
50°F	10°C	122°F	50°C
59°F	15°C	212°F	100°C

Useful Conversions

Good Cooking Rules

When handling and cooking foods, there are a few rules and guidelines that should be observed so that food remains fit to eat and uncontaminated with the bacteria and bugs that can result in food poisoning.

Good Hygiene Rules

~ Personal hygiene is imperative when handling food. Before commencing, wash hands thoroughly with soap, taking particular care with nails. Always wash hands after going to the toilet. Wash again after handling raw foods, cooked meats or vegetables. Do not touch any part of the body or handle pets, rubbish or dirty washing during food preparation.

~ Cuts should be covered with a waterproof plaster, preferably blue so it can be easily seen if lost.

~ Keep all surfaces clean using antibacterial cleanser and clean cloths.

~ Ensure that hair is off the face and does not trail into food or machinery.

~ Use a dishwasher wherever possible and wash utensils and equipment in very hot, soapy water.

~ Use clean dish cloths and tea towels, replacing regularly or boiling them to kill any bacteria.

~ Chopping boards and cooking implements must be clean. Boards should either be washed in a dishwasher or scrubbed after each use. Keep a separate board for meat, fish and vegetables and wash knives before using on different types of food. Use separate boards for raw and cooked food or wash them thoroughly in-between.

- Use dustbin liners for rubbish and empty regularly, cleaning your bin with disinfectant. Dustbins should be outside.

Guidelines for Using a Refrigerator

- Ensure that the refrigerator is situated away from any equipment that gives off heat, such as the cooker, washing machine or tumble drier, to ensure the greatest efficiency. Ensure that the vents are not obstructed.

- If not frost-free, defrost regularly, wiping down with a mild solution of bicarbonate of soda dissolved in warm water and a clean cloth.

- Close the door as quickly as possible so that the motor does not have to work overtime to keep it at the correct temperature.

- Ensure that the temperature is 5°C. A thermometer is a good investment.

- Avoid over-loading – this just makes the motor work harder.

- Cool food before placing in the refrigerator and always cover to avoid any smells or transference of taste to other foods.

- Remove supermarket packaging from raw meat, poultry and fish, place on a plate or dish, cover loosely and store at the base of the refrigerator to ensure that the juices do not drip on other foods.

- Store cheese in a box or container, wrapped to prevent the cheese drying out.

- Remove food to be eaten raw 30 minutes before use so it can return to room temperature.

- Cooked meats, bacon and all cooked dishes should be stored at the top – this is the coldest part.

Good Cooking Rules

- Store eggs in the egg compartment and remove 30 minutes before cooking in order to return them to temperature.

- Butter and all fats can be stored on the door, as can milk, cold drinks, sauces, mayonnaise and preserves with low sugar content.

- Cream and other dairy products, as well as pastries such as chocolate éclairs, should be stored on the middle shelf.

- Vegetables, salad and fruit should be stored in the salad boxes at the bottom of the refrigerator.

- Soft fruits should be kept in the salad box along with mushrooms, which are best kept in paper bags.

- To avoid cross-contamination, raw and cooked foods must be stored separately.

- Use all foods by the sell-by date – once opened, treat as cooked foods and use within two days.

Freezing Rules and Tips

- When buying frozen foods, transport in freezer-insulated bags, placing in the freezer as soon as possible after purchase.

- Do not re-freeze any thawed frozen foods unless cooked first.

- Date and label frozen food and use in rotation.

- Ensure that all food is thoroughly thawed before use, unless meant to be cooked from frozen.

- Freezer bags can be better for smaller spaces, as they use less space than containers.

➣ Do not attempt to home freeze any large joints or chickens. The domestic freezer does not reach a low enough temperature fast enough, so toxins may start to grow.

Open Freezing

Some food, such as individual portions of fish, meat or cake, benefits from being frozen individually rather than being put into a bag to freeze. This is called open freezing. Simply put the items to be frozen on a tray lined with nonstick baking paper, ensuring that they do not touch each other. Place in the freezer and freeze until completely frozen. Pack into a freezer bag or container, label and date before returning to the freezer as quickly as possible. When wishing to defrost a portion, remove from the bag or container and place on a plate and allow to thaw. Do not add other food to the original frozen food at a later date.

Freezing Rice

It is possible to freeze rice but experts advise home cooks against it because it contains harmful spores that cannot be killed by reheating. If still wishing to freeze rice, the best method is to cool it very quickly after cooking. Place a thin layer on a tray and cover to help cool the rice. Once cool, place into freezer bags and freeze. To use, thaw, then reheat to at least 75°C for 2 minutes, then eat. Do not freeze again.

Defrosting Freezers

It is important that the freezer is defrosted at least every 6 months and the cabinet is cleaned inside and out. This ensures that there are no packages lurking at the back or bottom of the freezer and the risk of passing toxins onto fresh frozen food is kept to a minimum. Use old towels and trays to mop up and collect the water, emptying the trays regularly. Clean the inside of the cabinet and drawers or trays with a solution of bicarbonate of soda and warm water. Use 1 tablespoon of bicarbonate of soda to 1.1 litres/2 pints warm water. Dry with a clean cloth and allow to reach the correct temperature before placing any food in the freezer.

General Rules

∾   Use all foods by the use-by date and store correctly whether fresh, frozen, canned or dried. Potatoes are best if removed from polythene, stored in brown paper and kept in the cool and dark.

∾   Cook all poultry thoroughly at the correct temperature (190°C/375°F/Gas Mark 5) ensuring that the juices run clear.

∾   Leave foods to cool as quickly as possible before placing in the refrigerator, and cover while cooling.

∾   Only reheat dishes once and always reheat thoroughly until piping hot. Remember to allow foods to stand when using the microwave and stir to distribute the heat.

∾   Microwaves vary according to make and wattage – always refer to manufacturer's instructions.

∾   Ensure that eggs are fresh. The elderly, pregnant women, those with a recurring illness, toddlers and babies should not be given mayonnaise, soufflés or other dishes that use raw or semi-cooked egg.

∾   Chilled foods, such as cold meats, cheese, fresh meat, fish and dairy products should be bought, taken home and placed in the refrigerator immediately. Do not keep in a warm car or room.

∾   Do not buy eggs or frozen or chilled foods that are damaged in any way and always avoid buying damaged or unlabelled canned goods. Keep store cupboards clean, wiping down regularly and rotating the food.

∾   Flour, nuts, rice, pulses, grains and pasta should be checked regularly and, once opened, placed in airtight containers.

∾   Keep dried herbs and ready-ground spices in a cool, dark place. They quickly lose their pungency and flavour when exposed to light.

Nutrition

ठ

Good nutrition is essential at any time – especially when you may be still growing and need to keep up with the rigours of study and socialising. Our bodies need a variety of different foods in order for them to work properly and for us to remain healthy. Food on a budget does not mean that nutritious food and well-balanced meals are off the agenda. Food should have flavour and look great, but it should be good for us too.

What are Nutrients?

These are chemical compounds that are present in food. They supply energy for the body and help build and replace cells. They also help to regulate our bodies' processes. Not including water, there are five categories of nutrients: carbohydrates, fats, proteins, vitamins and minerals. To this list you could also add 'fibre'. This is not really a nutrient as such, but is nevertheless very necessary for a healthy, functioning body.

What About Calories?

A calorie (written as 'kcal' on food labels) is just a measurement of energy. It is actually defined as the amount of heat needed to raise the temperature of 1 kg of water by 1°C. We need this energy, but there is enormous debate about how many calories adult humans need to eat every day in order to remain healthy. Broadly, men need around 2,700 calories a day and women about 2,000. Up to 60 per cent of those calories can come from carbohydrates, 20 per cent from proteins and up to 20 per cent from fats.

ठ   Nutrition

Calorie Content in Carbohydrate, Protein and Fat

Without sufficient food energy a body cannot function properly. So how many calories can the three basic nutritional elements give you?

- **Carbohydrate** 1 oz (28 g) of carbohydrate contains 112 calories.

- **Protein** The same amount of protein contains 112 calories.

- **Fat** The same amount of fat contains 252 calories.

Food from animals tends to be higher in fat, and some products, such as fruit, vegetables and grains are naturally low in fat. But beware, because some grocery items like French fries or croissants are prepared with fat.

Carbohydrates

These are an important source of food energy. Carbohydrates exist in two forms: complex and simple. Complex carbohydrates, which contain starches and fibre, are the best as they provide a slower-burning and thus more constant supply of energy. Complex carbohydrates that contain refined starches are not so good for you, however. Simple carbohydrates are sugars. Some are natural whilst others are refined – again, the refined kind are particularly bad for you. Examples of foods that contain carbohydrates are:

- **Complex carbohydrates (starches)** Brown rice; wholemeal breads, grains, cereals, flour and pasta; beans and peas; root vegetables; bananas.

- **Complex carbohydrates (refined starches)** White bread, flour, pasta and rice; processed breakfast cereals; pizzas; biscuits, pastries and cakes.

- Simple carbohydrates (sugars) The natural ones are in fruit and vegetables. Even these can cause tooth decay.

- Simple carbohydrates (refined sugars) Chocolate; honey; jams; soft drinks; sweets and snacks; prepared food and sauces; biscuits, cakes and pastries.

Fibre

Fibre is basically carbohydrate that the body cannot use, so it does not supply the body with energy. However, it is essential in helping the intestinal tract to work properly and flush out waste. Dietary fibre can also prevent some kinds of cancer. It can be found in whole grains and fruit and vegetables, provided they are eaten raw.

Fats

Cholesterol (an element of animal fat) is often portrayed as the developed world's health time bomb. It is linked to heart disease and it is found in a wide variety of food, such as beef, pork, poultry, butter, egg yolks, liver, shellfish and dairy products. However, cholesterol is an important part of a healthy body and it is only when it reaches high levels in the blood that it becomes a danger. In fact, fat in general is a very necessary element of the diet, but some are better than others:

- Saturated fats These are fats that are solid at room temperature. You find them in dairy products, animal fats, fatty meat, some oils and foods such as chocolate. These are the ones that contribute to health problems.

- Polyunsaturated fats Found in fish and soybean, and sunflower, corn and safflower oils. They are considered to be more healthy options.

- Monounsaturated fats These can be found in olive oil and whole grains and nuts. These too are considered to be more healthy.

Nutrition

∾ Trans fats Trans fats are certain types of unsaturated fat that can be polyunsaturated or monounsaturated, but which have become more like saturated fat, usually by virtue of a process of partial hydrogenation. Trans fats have been linked to an elevated risk of coronary heart disease, so it is advisable to avoid foods (typically processed foods) which contain partially hydrogenated vegetable oils.

Proteins

Proteins are amino acids necessary for complicated functions within our cells. The body can make its own amino acids, but there are eight types that it can't make so we need to get them from food. This is why we need to have dairy products, poultry, fish, eggs and meat in our diet. Proteins are essential for energy and building body tissue.

Vitamins and Minerals

Both of these are essential but neither contains energy. Key vitamins and minerals, and examples of what foods contain them are as follows:

∾ Vitamin A Contained in mango, broccoli, squashes, carrots and pumpkins.

∾ Vitamin B Contained in spinach, peas, tomato, water melon and potatoes.

∾ Vitamin C Contained in spinach, peppers, kiwi fruit, strawberries and citrus fruits.

∾ Vitamin D Contained in egg yolks, liver and oily fish.

∾ Vitamin E Contained in wheat germ, avocado, sweet potatoes and tofu.

∾ Vitamin K Contained in leafy green vegetables, broccoli, cabbage and liver.

- **Calcium** A mineral contained in milk, cheese and sardines.

- **Iron** A mineral contained in artichokes, spinach and clams.

- **Iodine** A mineral contained in salt, seafood, bread and milk.

- **Sodium** The easiest way to take in the mineral sodium is through salt, but not too much because it causes high blood pressure. It is also in soy sauce, bread and milk.

- **Potassium** A mineral contained in potatoes, green beans and bananas.

The Balanced Diet

You don't need to know the science behind nutrition, simply aim for a balanced diet and your body should receive everything it needs. The plate concept shown on page 17 shows the proportions in which you should eat the different food groups, but mainly just follow some golden rules:

- **Variety:** Eat a variety of foods to provide your body with everything it needs.

- **Exercise:** Balance your food with physical activity to improve fitness.

- **Natural and wholesome:** Eat plenty of whole grains, vegetables and fruit.

- **Keep a check on fats:** Avoid saturated fats to keep your cholesterol down.

- **Keep a check on sugars:** Don't include too many sugars in your diet.

- **Keep a check on salt:** Reduce the amount of salt and sodium to below 6 g a day to avoid high blood pressure. Remember that high salt quantities may be hiding in processed foods.

- **Drink alcohol in moderation:** It supplies calories but little or no nutrients.

Tools & Equipment

C

In this section, I have listed the tools and equipment you will need in order to start cooking, Some of the tools and equipment are absolutely essential and I would recommend that you invest in these first. Other less-essential tools and equipment can also be reasonably expensive, so they might be good ideas to suggest as either birthday or Christmas presents.

Essential Tools

∿ **Knives** Knives are perhaps the most important tools in the kitchen. It is advisable to have a good selection. First, when buying, make sure that any knife sits comfortably in your hand. You will need a small knife (often called a 'paring' knife) for all the little jobs, such as deseeding a chilli and cutting fruits and vegetables into small pieces. At least a further three to four additional knives would be good: a large chef's knife, which has a long wide blade, is ideal for chopping both meat and fish as well as fresh herbs; a carving knife; a bread knife, with or without a serrated edge; and a medium-sized all-purpose knife for all other jobs. Make sure that the knives are a reputable brand and easy to sharpen – a good knife will last a long while, maybe for ever.

∿ **Wooden Spoons** I feel you can never have too many wooden spoons! Although they will not last for ever, looked after and washed properly they should last for at least one to two years, depending on what you use them for. I would recommend buying one of the sets that are so readily available. These normally come in different lengths – the shorter one is super for sauces and the other two for stirring food, such as meat that is being sealed in a pan, as well as for mixing cakes and batters. Although they wash perfectly well, it is a good idea to keep some spoons for sweet dishes and others for savoury dishes. Then there are the wooden spatulas which are perfect for omelettes or frying meats such as chops, as the flat, wider area makes turning food over so much easier.

- **Large Spoons** These can be a plain spoon, ideal for stirring or dishing out casseroles, stews and vegetables, or a slotted draining spoon – this refers to the gaps in the bowl of the spoon which allow any liquid to drain out, back into the pan, for example, when removing meat after sealing it for a stew or casserole.

- **Measuring Spoons** These ensure that the correct amount of an ingredient is used (such as 1/4 teaspoon or 1 tablespoon). This is especially useful when either following a specific diet (for example, where oil and butter intake needs to be measured), or for use with a thickening agent such as cornflour, or with spices, where too much could completely ruin the dish.

- **Spatula** Also known as a 'fish slice', this is not the more ornate, usually silver utensil, used when serving fish in front of guests, but the plastic or metal utensil with slotted holes that is superb for turning food over and for removing cooked food from hot baking trays or roasting tins – plastic is kinder on nonstick pans but may not be as durable. They also come in wooden versions, which are normally narrower with a slightly slanted or flat base.

- **Vegetable Peeler** Using a peeler makes the job easier and will ensure that you get an even look to the peeled fruit or vegetable, such as peeling pears for cooking in wine or peeling potatoes. I prefer the swivel-blade peeler as it only removes a very thin layer and this will mean that, since many of the nutrients are just below the skin, they are preserved. However, it is a matter of personal choice, so when buying, try imitating the peeling action and see which fits you most comfortably.

- **Grater** For grating cheese, carrots and other root vegetables, fresh root ginger, chocolate, citrus zest and nutmeg – those last two should be done on the finest side of the grater.

Extra Tools

- **Ladle** Perfect for hot soups, casseroles, stews and any other hot liquids that need transferring or serving.

- **Potato Masher** You would be quite stuck without this if you wanted to make mashed potatoes, and it is handy for chunky soups too. It is superb for mashing all manner of vegetables, from potatoes to parsnips, carrots, yams or sweet potatoes.

- **Kebab Sticks and Skewers** Not essential at all – unless you want to make kebabs! Either metal or wooden, kebab sticks are for cooking both savoury and sweet kebabs, koftas and satays, and skewering fish or chicken into 'spatchcock' shape – this is where the food is split almost in half, then skewered to keep its shape prior to cooking. Remember that wooden kebab sticks need soaking in cold water for at least 30 minutes and both ends wrapped in kitchen foil to prevent the ends from burning and the cook burning her or his fingers. Skewers are similar to kebab sticks but are always made of metal. They can be used for kebabs but are also perfect for testing whether cakes are cooked in the middle, or if poultry is completely cooked – especially when cooking turkeys, as the very long skewers will go right through the thickest part straight to the centre cavity.

- **Whisks** Used for whisking eggs, whipping cream or sauces in order to create a smooth consistency and incorporate air. They are usually formed from interlocking wires and are available in various types, most commonly the balloon whisk of varying sizes, the mechanically hand-operated rotary whisk and a flat whisk. All work well but take longer than one powered by electricity – *see* page 30.

Basic Equipment

Certain pieces of equipment are essential when cooking. There is no need to go out and spend a fortune, as most of the equipment is relatively cheap. However, what I would recommend is that you buy good quality pans, ones that will not buckle in the heat after being used a couple of times. Nonstick pans can also make life a lot easier when it comes to the washing up. Below is a list of equipment that will start the beginner cook on their way and can easily be added to after a little time and some experience is gained.

∾ Chopping Boards Essential for any job that involves cutting. Look for the colour co-ordinated boards, so that you can use a different colour for different types of food (that is, to keep meat, especially chicken, separate from vegetables, for example). That way, there will be no cross-contamination of food. Make sure that you wash them thoroughly after use, washing in the dishwasher if you have one.

∾ Measuring Jug Essential for measuring liquids, with the measurements marked down the side of the jug. These are available in different sizes and again can be bought as glass Pyrex jugs or in plastic.

∾ Scales These are essential in British cooking, especially when baking. Most scales, whether digital or conventional, measure in both grams and ounces, and all have a bowl in which to place the ingredients to be measured.

∾ Mixing Bowls Ideally, you will have at least three – in small, medium and large. These can be Pyrex glass or similar and are essential for many jobs in the kitchen, including soaking, storing, creaming butter and sugar for cakes, pastry making, melting chocolate, whipping cream and whisking egg whites.

∾ Pans Perhaps the most expensive investment when first beginning to cook. I would recommend that you buy a set of saucepans, as normally there are three to five of differing sizes and these should be adequate to begin with. A good frying pan is important, preferably with a lid to increase its versatility. You might also like to have a milk (small) pan for making sauces as well as boiling milk.

∾ Colander and Sieve Used for sifting flours and straining ingredients to remove any lumps, a sieve is usually made of fine mesh wire, while a colander tends to be rather bigger, with bigger holes or slots, and is used for draining cooked pasta and vegetables. The latter come in plastic and metal versions.

∾ Baking Trays Those without edges all round are often referred to as 'sheets'. Baking trays have many varied uses. Dishes such as lasagne can be placed on baking trays so that they are

easy to place in the oven as well as remove. They are also good for baking such items as scones, meringues and cookies as well as using to reheat dishes. Other baking equipment can be bought as it is required; to begin with, I would suggest that you keep it to the minimum with one or two baking trays.

Clingfilm, Food Boxes and Bags You are bound to have leftovers that you do not want to waste, so it is essential that you have clingfilm for covering food to be put in the fridge, a few freezer-safe plastic boxes with securely fitting lids and some plastic freezer bags – as we have said, freezer bags can be better if you're tight on space, as they take up less room in your freezer than solid containers.

Extra Equipment

- **Handheld Blender** Out of the items in this list, this is the cheapest and easiest and thus the first and only one that a student should consider buying. Also known as immersion blenders, they can be bought for less than a tenner in big supermarkets, and do the job well and conveniently – ideal if you plan to make soups.

- **Blender or Liquidiser** Very similar to a food processor, having a jug rather than a bowl. Blends and chops but does not do all the jobs that a food processor will do.

- **Food Mixer** These can be freestanding and perform many jobs in the kitchen from whipping cream, whisking egg whites, creaming butter and sugar for baking cakes to making dough for bread and rubbing in pastry, or simply placing all the ingredients in the bowl and mixing. Smaller, cheaper hand-held versions are available, which you may greatly appreciate if you plan to make more than the odd cake – hand whisking and beating can be tiring after a while!

- **Food Processor** A very versatile piece of equipment and one that I would recommend keen cooks investing in – but perhaps a few years down the line. It will chop vegetables, fruit, nuts and herbs, and shred vegetables, as well as blend soups, make pastry dough and even cakes. Available at different prices.

Terminology

Over the years, the language of cooking has developed and now there are many new words and expressions, which perhaps twenty-five years ago no one would have dreamt of using in connection with cooking. In any case, below are some of the basic words you are likely to come across.

∾ **Al dente** Used to describe pasta when it is cooked to the desired amount – that is, tender but still firm to the bite. It is important not to overcook pasta.

∾ **Baking** Cooking foods in the oven. This normally applies primarily to cakes, breads, pastries and puddings, but can refer to anything cooked in the dry heat of the oven. 'Baking' is often used interchangeably with 'roasting', but a distinction can arguably be drawn by saying that 'roasting' implies greater heat and more pronounced browning. 'Roasting' is also the preferred term for meat, poultry and vegetables, while 'baking' tends to be reserved for fish, seafood and the items mentioned above.

∾ **Basting** Brushing or drizzling meat or fish with its own juices, oil or a prepared sauce, while roasting or grilling, to add flavour and retain moisture.

∾ **Beating** Using a wooden spoon to mix ingredients together until smooth, such as when making batter for pancakes or Yorkshire pudding.

∾ **Blanching** Pouring boiling water over fresh green vegetables (or immersing them into boiling water for a short time) in order to preserve the colour. They are then typically plunged into cold water to halt the cooking process. This is done when vegetables are either to be frozen or added to a dish towards the end of cooking. It will also speed up their cooking time.

- **Bruising** Slightly crushing an ingredient, usually with the flat side of a chef's knife or a rolling pin, in order to release its flavour.

- **Creaming** Beating butter or margarine with sugar until lighter in colour and soft and creamy in texture. This applies to cake making.

- **Drizzling** Pouring a little sauce or oil over food while taking care not to swamp it.

- **Dropping consistency** This applies in particular to sponges. The finished unbaked mixture should gently fall off the wooden spoon when it is lightly tapped on the edge of the bowl.

- **En papillote** Food wrapped in paper – usually baking parchment – and cooked in the oven. The dish is normally served still in the paper so that, on opening, the eater gets the full aroma from the spices and flavours used.

- **Flaking** Separating fish into fine flakes.

- **Folding in** This applies to stirring another ingredient into an uncooked mixture such as a meringue or sponge cake mixture. Care must be taken that the mixture is not overmixed, as this will remove the air that has been whisked in, thus preventing a good rise or the required light texture.

- **Frying** Cooking fresh food in, normally, a frying pan or, sometimes, a deep-fat fryer, cooking it to a certain stage or completely. Food is fried in oil or fat until cooked (fats include dripping, lard, margarine, ghee and butter).

- **Glazing** Brushing a food with egg, butter or other liquid, sometimes prior to cooking, to give a good colour or to enhance the finished dish.

- **Infusing** Liquids are heated gently with seasonings or flavours, then left for the flavours to develop in the liquid.

- **Julienne** The style of cut whereby vegetables or zest are cut into very thin strips, often for garnish.

- **Jus** The natural juices from cooking meat, often used as a gravy. The word is also used to mean a slightly more elaborate kind of sauce reduction based on the 'jus'.

- **Kneading** This applies mainly to pastry and bread. The just-made dough is placed on a floured surface. Using the knuckles, the dough is stretched and folded over on itself until smooth. This stretches the dough and makes it more elastic and pliable.

- **Reduction** The process and result of boiling a liquid to both reduce the amount and to make the flavour more intense.

- **Refreshing** Plunging vegetables into cold water to stop the cooking process and to preserve the colour. The vegetables are normally reheated before serving.

- **Roux** A cooked butter and flour paste, normally in equal quantities, used to thicken sauces. Small amounts are added to simmering liquid and whisked in, or the roux is made in a small pan and warm liquid stirred in, then the pan is placed over a gentle heat and cooked, stirring, until thickened.

- **Sautéing** This simply means frying, and refers mainly to the cooking of meat and vegetables in a frying pan when first starting to cook in order to seal in the meat juices and help preserve their nutrients and flavour.

- **Scoring** Making cuts into pork or gammon rind, both for decorative effect and to help the food cook more quickly.

- **Searing** Cooking meat or other foods very quickly under the grill or in the oven in order to seal in the juices and to give a golden brown appearance.

- **Sifting** Shaking icing sugar or flour through a sieve, to remove any lumps and to aerate in order to help with the rising of cakes.

- **Simmering** When liquid is brought to the boil, then the heat is reduced so that a few bubbles gently break the surface. If the bubbles do not appear, increase the heat slightly.

- **Steaming** A method of cooking food with steam, rather than directly in water. Vegetables are especially good if steamed, as most of the nutrients are preserved and not lost into the water, as happens when they are boiled. Food is placed in a container that will allow the steam to pass through, which sits on top of a pan with gently simmering water. The steamer is covered with a lid.

- **Whipping** This is when whipping or double cream is beaten with a whisk until soft peaks are formed in the thickened cream. Can be whipped either by machine or by a handheld whisk such as a balloon whisk.

- **Whisking** Beating with a whisk – usually egg whites, either with a food mixer or using a handheld whisk, until the egg white is stiff and dry (this means that the bowl of whisked egg whites can be tipped upside down and the egg white does not move).

- **Zest** What is the difference between 'zest' and 'rind'? 'Zest' is the outermost part of the 'rind' of a citrus fruit, as opposed to the white 'pith' underneath, but in a cooking context can refer to the long thin strips of zest made with a 'zester' (which are used for decoration only, as, if eaten, will give a bitter taste) or to grated zest, which is made by rubbing the unpeeled but washed or scrubbed fruit up and down the fine side of a grater, giving very fine pieces. As these are thinner than zest strips, they can be used to flavour dishes.

Store Cupboard Essentials

The first food shopping trip should be focused on setting up a well-targeted store cupboard. There are lots of ingredients that you can expect to use again and again but which you should not have to buy on a frequent basis.

When thinking about essentials, think of flavour, something that is going to add to a dish without increasing its fat content. It is worth spending a bit more money on these products to make flavoursome dishes that will help stop the urge to snack on fatty foods.

What to Stock in Your Store Cupboard

Store the ingredients in a cool, dark place and remember to rotate them. Most will be safe to use for six months.

∞ **Herbs and spices** Certain key herbs and spices are essential for flavoursome food. Often it is preferable to use fresh herbs and freshly ground spices, but the dried and ready-ground varieties have their merits. Dried herbs and spices keep well and are cheaper – keep them in a cool, dark place, not exposed to sunlight. Using herbs when cooking at home should reduce the temptation to buy ready-made sauces. Often these types of sauces contain large amounts of sugar and additives. Some key dried herbs and spices to purchase are: bay leaves, thyme, oregano, parsley, mixed herbs, spices, ground cinnamon, cumin, ground coriander, crushed chillies, ground ginger, mixed spice, curry powder and turmeric.

∾ Pasta Whether fresh (it can also be frozen) or dried, pasta is a versatile ingredient with which to provide the body with slow-release energy. It comes in many different sizes and shapes; from the tiny tubettini (which can be added to soups to create a more substantial dish), to penne, fusilli, rigatoni and conchiglie, up to the larger cannelloni and lasagne sheets and, of course, spaghetti. (*See* also page 45.)

∾ Noodles Also very useful and can accompany any Far Eastern dish. They are low fat and also available in the wholemeal variety. Rice noodles are available for those who have gluten-free diets; like pasta, they provide slow-release energy to the body.

∾ Rice When cooked, rice swells to create a substantial low-fat dish. Basmati and Thai fragrant rice are well suited to Indian and Thai curries, as the fine grains absorb the sauce and their delicate creaminess balances the pungency of the spices. Arborio is only one type of risotto rice – many are available, depending on whether the risotto is meant to accompany meat, fish or vegetables. Long-grain is perhaps the most popular and versatile of rice and is perfect for both rich and simple dishes. Having a subtle flavour, it is milled to remove the husk and bran layer. On cooking, the grains separate to give a fluffy texture. Also available as brown long-grain. Easy-cook long-grain rice, both white and brown, is great for casseroles and for stuffing meat, fish and vegetables, as it holds its shape and firmness.

Pudding rice can be used in a variety of ways to create an irresistible dessert. Rice will keep for several years if kept in sealed packets. However, it is at its best when fresh. To ensure freshness, always buy rice from reputable shops with a good turnover and buy in small quantities. Once opened, store the rice in an airtight container in a cool, dry place to keep out moisture.

Although there are many varieties of rice readily available, it is not necessary to have them all. To begin with why not buy either white or brown basmati rice, Thai fragrant rice if you intend to cook a lot of stir-fries and long-grain rice, which is a versatile rice and can be used for most dishes.

- **Couscous** Not essential, but you may like to use this occasionally. Now available in instant form, couscous just needs to be covered with boiling water, then forked. Couscous is a precooked wheat semolina. Traditional couscous needs to be steamed and is available from health food stores and supermarkets. This type of couscous contains more nutrients than the instant variety.

- **Bulgur wheat** Also not essential. A cracked wheat that is often used in tabbouleh. Bulgur wheat is a good source of complex carbohydrate.

- **Pulses/beans** A vital ingredient for the store cupboard, pulses – which include beans such as kidney, borlotti, cannellini, butter and flageolet, as well as split peas and lentils – are easy to store, have a very high nutritional value and are great when added to soups, casseroles, curries and hotpots. Pulses also act as a thickener, whether flavoured or on their own.

Beans come in two forms: either dried (in which case they need to be soaked overnight and then some must be boiled for 10 minutes before use – it is important to follow the packet instructions), or canned, which although more expensive is a convenient time-saver because dried pulses take time to prepare. When boiling previously dried pulses, remember that salt should not be added as this will make the skins tough and inedible. If buying canned pulses, try to buy the variety in water with no added salt or sugar. These simply need to be drained and rinsed before being added to a dish.

- **Dried fruit** The ready-to-eat variety are particularly good as they are plump, juicy and do not need to be soaked. They are fantastic when puréed into a compote, added to water and heated to make a pie filling and when added to stuffing mixtures. They are also good cooked with meats, rice or couscous.

❧ Flours Apart from cornflour and perhaps a little plain flour, since both are used for thickening sauces, you may not need to stock flour unless you intend to bake. It is worth mentioning that wholemeal flour should not be stored for too long at room temperature as the fats may turn rancid.

❧ Cooking oil It is recognised that olive oil is the best oil to use both for health properties and taste. If intending only to cook with olive oil, then buy 'mild', 'medium' or 'blended for cooking' olive oil; if using it for salad dressing or to drizzle, then invest in a bottle of extra virgin olive oil too (do not cook with it).

However, there other oils which are still healthy to use and are cheaper. Try vegetable oil, which can be used for all methods of cooking, has a distinct flavour and is reasonably priced, as is sunflower oil, which is more delicate and a lighter oil. Or try rapeseed oil, corn oil or groundnut oil, which is usually used in Eastern cooking. Speciality oils, such as sesame, walnut, herb and spiced flavoured oils are expensive and are reserved mainly to add extra flavour at the end of cooking or for salad or vegetable dressings.

❧ Stock Good-quality stock is a must in low-fat cooking, as it provides a good flavour base for many dishes. Many supermarkets now carry a variety of fresh and organic stocks, which, although they need refrigeration, are probably one of the most time- and effort-saving ingredients available. There is also a fairly large range of dried stock, perhaps the best being bouillon, a high-quality form of stock (available in powder or liquid form) which can be added to any dish, whether it be a sauce, casserole, pie or soup.

Sauce ingredients Many people favour meals that can be prepared and cooked in 30–45 minutes, so helpful ingredients that kick-start a sauce are great. A good-quality passata sauce or canned tomatoes, which are almost as good as passata but cheaper, can act as the foundation for any sauce, as can a good-quality green or red pesto (though pesto can be great to make from scratch). Other handy store cupboard additions include tapenade, mustard and anchovies. These have very distinctive tastes and are particularly flavoursome. Roasted red pepper sauce and sun-dried tomato paste, which tends to be sweeter and more intensely flavoured than regular tomato purée, are also very useful.

Vinegar This is another worthwhile store-cupboard essential and, with so many uses, it might be worth splashing out on really good-quality wine vinegar or even a balsamic vinegar.

Sauces and flavours Eastern flavourings such as fish sauce, soy sauce, red and green curry paste, chilli sauce and Chinese rice wine all offer mouthwatering flavours to any dish. For those who are incredibly short on time, or who rarely shop, it is now possible to purchase a selection of ready-prepared freshly minced garlic, ginger and chilli (available in jars which can be kept in the refrigerator). Mustard and ketchup, which you may use in your sarnies, can also be handy in cooking.

Alcohol You are not going to be flambéing or cooking with expensive brandy, but since you may be partial to the odd glass of wine or pint of beer, then why not use any leftovers in risottos and stews?

Canned foods Canned ingredients can be just as good quality as fresh, at half the price and with a long shelf life – some are more reliable than others however. Top of the list are canned tomatoes, swiftly followed by tuna, sardines, anchovies, olives, sweetcorn, beans, baked beans and perhaps corned beef.

Store Cupboard Essentials

Cooking Eggs

No other food is as versatile in cooking as the egg – it is used in many diverse ways and is an essential ingredient for all good cooks. But first things first: here are some of the basic and essential ways to cook eggs.

Boiled Eggs

Eggs should be boiled in gently simmering water. Remove the egg from the refrigerator at least 30 minutes before cooking.

1. Bring a pan of water to the boil, then, once boiling, lower the heat to a simmer.

2. Gently lower the egg into the water and cook for 3 minutes for lightly set, or 4 minutes for a slightly firmer set.

3. Remove and lightly tap to stop the egg continuing to cook.

4. Serve lightly boiled eggs with toast or buttered bread cut into fingers to use as dippers.

   Hard-boiled eggs should be cooked for 10 minutes, then plunged into cold water and left until cold before shelling.

Fried Eggs

1. Put a little sunflower oil or butter in a frying pan and heat.

2. Break an egg into a cup or small jug. Carefully slip into the pan.

3. Cook, spooning the hot oil or fat over the egg, for 3–4 minutes until set to personal preference.

4. Remove with a palette knife or fish slice.

5. Serve with freshly grilled bacon or sausages, or on toast with baked beans and tomatoes.

Poached Eggs

1. Half-fill a frying pan with water. Bring to a gentle boil, then reduce the heat to a simmer.

2. Add either a little salt or a few drops of vinegar or lemon juice – this will help the egg to retain its shape.

3. Break the egg into a cup or small jug and carefully slip into the simmering water. Lightly oiled round, plain pastry cutters can be used to contain the eggs, if preferred.

4. Cover the pan with a lid and cook for 3–4 minutes until set to personal preference.

5. Once cooked, remove by draining with a fish slice or flat spatula.

6. Serve either on hot buttered toast or on top of sliced ham or freshly cooked spinach.

Cooking Eggs

Scrambled Eggs

For sufficient scrambled eggs, allow two eggs per person.

1. Melt 1 tablespoon butter or margarine in a small pan.

2. Break the eggs into a small bowl and add 1 tablespoon milk and seasoning to taste. Whisk with a fork until blended, then pour into the melted butter or margarine.

3. Cook over a gentle heat, stirring with a wooden spoon, until set and creamy.

4. Serve on hot buttered toast with smoked salmon, if liked, or stir in some freshly snipped chives or chopped tomatoes.

Omelettes

For a basic omelette, allow two eggs per person. Add herbs and seasoning as desired.

1. Break the eggs into a small bowl, add seasoning to taste and 1 tablespoon milk. Whisk with a fork until frothy.

2. Heat 2 teaspoons oil in a frying pan and, when hot, pour in the egg mixture.

3. Cook gently, using a wooden spoon to bring the mixture from the edges of the pan to the centre and let the uncooked egg mixture flow to the edges.

4. When the egg has set, cook without moving it for an extra minute before folding the omelette into three and gently turning out onto a warmed serving plate. Take care not to overcook.

- Cheese Omelette Proceed as before, then sprinkle 25–40 g/1–1¹/₂ oz grated mature Cheddar cheese on top of the lightly set omelette. Cook for a further 2 minutes, or until the cheese starts to melt. If liked, place under a preheated grill for 2–3 minutes until golden. Fold and serve.

- Tomato Omelette Proceed as for a plain omelette. After 2 minutes of cooking time, add 1 chopped tomato on top of the omelette. Cook as above until set.

- Mushroom Omelette Wipe and slice 50 g/2 oz button mushrooms. Heat 1 tablespoon butter or margarine in a small pan and cook the mushrooms for 2–3 minutes. Drain and reserve. Cook the omelette as above, adding the mushrooms once set.

Separating Eggs

Occasionally a recipe may call for egg yolks or whites – to obtain these you need to literally separate the white from the yolk. Separate eggs as follows:

1. Crack an egg in half lightly and cleanly over a bowl, being careful not to break the yolk and keeping the yolk in the shell.

2. Tip the yolk backwards and forwards between the two shell halves, allowing as much of the white as possible to spill out into the bowl.

Keep or discard the yolk and/or the white as needed. Make sure that you do not get any yolk in your whites, as this will prevent successful whisking of the whites. It takes practice!

Cooking Eggs

Cooking Rice

℮

There are countless ways to cook rice, but much depends on the variety of rice being used, the dish being prepared and the desired results. Each variety of rice has its own unique characteristics. Some types of rice cook to light, separate grains, some to a rich, creamy consistency and some to a consistency where the grains stick together. Different types of rice have different powers of absorption.

Most rice (but not risotto) benefits from washing before cooking – tip into a sieve and rinse thoroughly under cold running water until the water runs clear. This removes any starch still clinging to the grains.

Long-grain Rice on the Hob

The simplest method of cooking long-grain rice is to add it to plenty of boiling, salted water in a large saucepan. Rice increases in size when cooked. As a guide allow 50 g/2 oz rice per person when cooking as an accompaniment or side dish, and slightly more if rice is acting as the main component of the meal.

1. Rinse under cold running water until clear, then tip into rapidly boiling water.

2. Stir the rice once, then, when the water has returned to the boil, reduce the heat and leave to simmer uncovered.

3. Allow 10–12 minutes for white rice and 30–40 minutes for brown – check the packet instructions for specific timings.

4. The easiest way to test if rice is cooked is to bite a couple of grains – they should be tender but still firm.

5. Drain immediately, return to the pan with a little butter and herbs, if liked. Fluff with a fork and serve.

   To keep the rice warm, put it in a bowl and place over a pan of barely simmering water. Cover the top of the bowl with a dishtowel until ready to serve.

∾ Absorption Method Cooking rice using the absorption method is also simple. Weigh out the quantity of rice, then measure it by volume using a measuring jug – you will need a volume of 150 ml/¼ pint for two people.

1. Rinse the rice, then tip into a large saucepan. If liked, cook the rice in a little butter or oil for 1 minute.

2. Pour in 2 parts water or stock to 1 part rice, season with salt and bring to the boil.

3. Cover, then simmer gently until the liquid is absorbed and the rice is tender. White rice will take 15 minutes to cook, whereas brown rice will take 35 minutes. If there is still a little liquid left when the rice is tender, uncover and cook for 1 minute until the liquid has evaporated.

4. Remove from the heat and leave covered for 4–5 minutes, then fluff up before serving.

Cooking Rice

Oven-baked Method

The oven-baked method works by absorption too, but takes longer than cooking on the hob. For oven-baked rice for two:

1. Fry a chopped onion in 1 tablespoon olive oil in a 1.1 litre/2 pint flameproof casserole dish until soft and golden.

2. Add 75 g/3 oz long-grain rice and cook for 1 minute.

3. Stir in 300 ml/^{1}/$_2$ pint stock – add a finely pared strip of lemon zest or a bay leaf, if liked.

4. Cover and bake in a preheated oven at 180°C/ 350°F/Gas Mark 4 for 40 minutes, or until the rice is tender and all the stock has been absorbed. Fluff up before serving.

Cooking in the Microwave

1. Place the rinsed long-grain rice in a large microwaveable bowl.

2. Add boiling water or stock, allowing 300 ml/^{1}/$_2$ pint for 125 g/ 4 oz rice and 500 ml/18 fl oz for 225 g/8 oz rice. Add a pinch of salt and a knob of butter, if desired.

3. Cover with pierced plastic wrap and cook on high for 3 minutes.

4. Stir, re-cover and cook on medium for 12 minutes for white rice and 25 minutes for brown.

5. Leave covered for 5 minutes before fluffing up and serving.

Cooking Pasta

though it is possible to make your own fresh pasta at home, few of us have the time or energy to do this, especially when fresh and dried pasta is so readily available to buy. In fact, although you may occasionally like to buy ready-made stuffed fresh pasta such as tortellini, there is no need to buy fresh pasta noodles or shapes – dried pasta is just as good, if not better, not to mention cheaper and long-lasting.

How to Cook Perfect Pasta

As an approximate guide, allow 75–125 g/3–4 oz uncooked pasta per person. The amount will depend on whether the pasta is being served for a light or main meal and the type of sauce that it is being served with. Follow a few simple rules to ensure that your pasta is cooked to perfection every time:

1. Choose a large saucepan – there needs to be plenty of room for the pasta to move around so it does not stick together.

2. Cook the pasta in a large quantity of fast-boiling, well-salted water, ideally 4 litres/ 7 pints water and 1½–2 tablespoons salt for every 350–450 g/12 oz–1 lb pasta.

3. Tip in the pasta all at once, stir and cover. Return to a rolling boil, then remove the lid. Once it is boiling, lower the heat to medium-high and cook the pasta for the required time. It should be *al dente* – in other words, tender but still firm to the bite.

4. Drain, reserving a little of the cooking water to stir into the drained pasta. This helps to thin the sauce, if necessary, and helps prevent the pasta sticking together as it cools.

Potatoes

༒

Potatoes are invaluable; they can be boiled, baked, mashed, roasted, chipped – what would we do without them? You may just buy the first or biggest ones you come across, but it may help you to know that potatoes are classified according to how early in the season they are ready for harvesting and are named as follows: first early, second early and maincrop.

The first earlies (such as the Maris Bard variety) are the first new potatoes on the market; they are very fresh and young and the skins can simply be rubbed off. The second earlies (such as Anya) are still new potatoes, but their skins will have begun to set. These potatoes will be difficult to scrape and are better cooked in their skins. Main crop potatoes (such as Maris Piper, King Edward, Charlotte, Désirée) are available all year round and may have been stored for several months.

Choosing

When buying potatoes, always choose ones with smooth, firm skins. When purchasing new potatoes, check that they are really young and fresh by scraping the skin – it should peel away very easily. Only buy the quantity you need and use within a couple of days.

Check maincrop potatoes to make sure that they are firm and not sprouting or showing any signs of mould. Avoid buying and discard any potatoes with greenish patches or carefully cut them out. These parts of the potato are toxic and a sign that they have been stored in light.

Storing

Potatoes should be stored in a cool, dark place but not in the refrigerator as the dampness will make them sweat, causing mould to grow. If the potatoes come in plastic bags, take them out and store in a paper bag or on a vegetable rack. If you prefer to buy in bulk, keep the potatoes in a cold, dark, dry place such as a larder or garage, making sure that they do not freeze in cold weather.

Sweet potatoes should be stored in a cool, dry place but, unlike ordinary potatoes, do not need to be kept in the dark.

Which Potato for Which Method?

Generally, new potato varieties have a firm and waxy texture that does not break up during cooking, so they are ideal for boiling, steaming and salads. Maincrop potatoes, on the other hand, have a more floury texture and lend themselves to mashing and roasting. Both types are suitable for chips. Individual potato varieties have their own characteristics. Some maincrop varieties are better for boiling than baking and vice versa, so choose the most appropriate type of potato for the dish being prepared (check the label or ask your retailer).

Whichever way you choose to serve your potatoes, allow 125–175 g/4–6 oz per person (about 4–6 new potatoes or 1–2 medium potatoes).

Boiled Potatoes

∾ New Potatoes Most of the new potatoes available nowadays are fairly clean – especially those sold in supermarkets – and simply need a light scrub before cooking in their skins.

1. If the potatoes are very dirty, use a small scrubbing brush or scourer to remove both the skins and dirt (or leave the skins on if they are second earlies, and peel when cooked, if liked).

2. Add them to a pan of cold, salted water and bring to the boil. Cover the pan with a lid and simmer for 12–15 minutes until tender. Very firm new potatoes can be simmered for 8 minutes, then left to stand in the hot water for a further 10 minutes until cooked through.

3. Add a couple of sprigs of fresh herbs to the pan if you like – fresh mint is traditionally used to flavour potatoes.

4. Drain the potatoes thoroughly and, if you want to peel them now, hold the hot potatoes with a fork to make this easier. Serve hot, tossed in a little melted butter or, for a change, a tablespoon of pesto.

∾ 'Old' (Maincrop) Potatoes

1. Choose a maincrop potato suitable for boiling, then peel thinly and cut into even-sized pieces. Alternatively, you can cook the potatoes in their skins and peel them after cooking.

2. Add to a saucepan of cold, salted water and bring to the boil. Cover the pan with a lid and simmer for 20 minutes, or until tender. Drain.

(It is particularly important to cook floury potatoes gently or the outsides may start to fall apart before they are tender in the centre. Drain the potatoes in a colander, then return them to the pan to dry out over a very low heat for 1–2 minutes.)

Mashed Potatoes

1. Boil your maincrop potatoes as described and, once cooked, roughly mash and add a knob of butter or margarine and 2 tablespoons of milk per person. Mash until smooth, with a hand masher, grater or a potato ricer.

2. Season to taste with salt, freshly ground black pepper and a little freshly grated nutmeg, if liked, then beat for a few seconds with a wooden spoon until fluffy.

As an alternative to butter or margarine, use a good-quality olive oil or crème fraîche. Finely chopped red and green chillies, crispy-cooked crumbled bacon, fresh herbs or grated Parmesan cheese can also be stirred in for additional flavour.

Steamed Potatoes

All potatoes are suitable for steaming. Floury potatoes, however, are ideal for this method of cooking, as they fall apart easily when boiled.

1. New and small potatoes can be steamed whole, but larger ones should be cut into even-sized pieces.

2. Place the potatoes in a steamer, colander or sieve over boiling water and cover. Steam for 10 minutes if the potatoes are small or, if they are cut into large chunks, cook for 20–25 minutes.

Chips

You are unlikely to deep-fry your own chips – ideally you'd need a deep-fat fryer; and lots of hot oil can be dangerous to use and onerous to replace. Of course you can buy frozen oven chips, but how about baking your own? It's lower fat than frying and less hassle.

1. Preheat the oven to 200°C/400°F/Gas Mark 6 and place a nonstick baking tray in the oven to heat up.

2. Cut the potatoes into 1.5 cm/⅝ inch slices, then cut the slices into long strips about 1.5 cm/⅝ inch wide to create classic chips, or cut your potatoes into chunky wedges, if preferred. Put the chips or wedges in a pan of cold water and quickly bring to the boil.

3. Simmer for 2 minutes, then drain in a colander. Leave for a few minutes to dry.

4. Drizzle over 1½–2 tablespoons of olive or sunflower oil and toss to coat.

5. Tip onto the heated baking tray and cook in the preheated oven for 20–25 minutes, turning occasionally, until golden brown and crisp.

Sautéed Potatoes

1. Cut peeled potatoes into rounds about 0.5 cm/¼ inch thick and pat dry.

2. Heat 25 g/1 oz/2 tbsp unsalted butter or margarine and 2 tablespoons oil in a large heavy-based frying pan until hot.

3. Add the potatoes in a single layer and cook for 4–5 minutes until the undersides are golden.

4. Turn with a large fish slice/spatula and gently cook the other side for 12–15 minutes until golden and tender.

5. Drain on paper towels and sprinkle with a little salt before serving.

Baked Potatoes

Allow a large (300–375 g/11–13 oz) potato per person and, if you can, choose a variety such as Maris Piper, Cara, King Edward, Russet Burbank or Russet Arcadia.

1. Wash and dry the potatoes, prick the skins lightly, then rub each one with a little oil and sprinkle with salt.

2. Bake at 200°C/400°F/Gas Mark 6 for 1–1¹/₂ hours until the skins are crisp and the centres are very soft. To speed up the cooking time, thread onto metal skewers, as this conducts heat to the middle of the potatoes.

Roast Potatoes

For crisp and brown outsides and fluffy centres, choose potatoes suitable for baking.

1. Thinly peel the potatoes and cut into even-sized pieces.

2. Drop into a pan of boiling, salted water and simmer for 5 minutes.

3. Turn off the heat and leave for a further 3–4 minutes.

4. Drain well and return the potatoes to the pan over a low heat for a minute to dry them and to roughen the edges.

5. Carefully transfer them to a roasting tin containing hot oil. Baste well, then bake at 220°C/425°F/Gas Mark 7 for 20 minutes.

6. Turn them and cook for a further 20–30 minutes, turning and basting at least one more time. Serve as soon as the potatoes are ready.

Potatoes

Microwaving Potatoes

The microwave can be used to boil new potatoes or peeled chunks of potato as follows:

1. To cook new potatoes in the microwave, prick the skins with a skewer to prevent them from bursting.

2. Place in a microwaveable bowl with 3 tablespoons boiling water.

3. Cover with clingfilm which has been pierced 2–3 times and cook on High for 12–15 minutes until tender.

You can also 'bake' potatoes in the microwave, providing you do not want the skins to be crispy:

1. Place each potato on a circle of paper towels. Make several cuts in each to ensure that the skins do not burst.

2. Transfer to the microwave plate and cook on High for 4–6 minutes per potato, allowing an extra 3–4 minutes for every additional potato. Turn the potatoes at least once during cooking.

3. Leave to stand for 5 minutes before serving.

Alternatively, get the best of both worlds by starting them off in the microwave for 4 minutes and then finishing them to a nice baked finish in the oven for 10–12 minutes. It may take rather longer if they are very big.

Meat, Poultry & Fish

Red Meat

Meat can be expensive, and, although it offers an excellent source of protein, B vitamins and iron, it also contains saturated fatty acids which are linked to raised blood cholesterol levels and increased risk of coronary heart disease. For this reason, it is now recommended that red meat is only eaten 2–3 times per week. Nonetheless, as a student you do not have to forego meat by any means.

- ∾ Cost Home-grown meat is normally more expensive than imported meat. Meat also varies in price, depending on the cut: the more expensive and tender meats are usually those cuts that exercised less. They need a minimal amount of cooking and are suitable for roasting, grilling, griddling, frying and stir-frying. The cheaper cuts, which are the belly, shoulder, neck, stewing meat (chuck or skirt, which is often sold as mince) and breast, such as lamb's, need longer, slower cooking and are used in casseroles and stews and for slow roasting. If you compare the price of mince made from skirt to the price of mince made from steak, such as rump, there is a big difference, but the cheaper skirt mince contains a lot of fat which needs cooking out.

- ∾ Choosing Look for meat that is lean without an excess of fat, is a good colour and has no unpleasant odour. If in doubt about the suitability of a cut, ask the butcher, who should be happy to advise.

~ Frozen Meat If buying frozen meat, allow to thaw before using. This is especially important for both pork and poultry (covered later). It is better to thaw meat slowly, lightly covered on the bottom shelf of the refrigerator. Use within 2–3 days of thawing, providing it has been kept in the refrigerator. If buying meat to freeze, do not freeze large joints in a home freezer, as it will not be frozen quickly enough.

~ Storing Store thawed or fresh meat out of the supermarket wrappings, on a plate, lightly covered with greaseproof or baking paper and then wrap with clingfilm, if liked. Do not secure the paper tightly round the meat, as it needs to breathe. Ensure that the raw meat juices do not drip onto cooked foods. The refrigerator needs to be at a temperature of 5°C/40°F. Fresh meat such as joints, chops and steaks can be stored for up to 3 days. Minced meats, sausages and offal should be stored for only 1 day.

~ Beef When choosing beef, look for meat that is a good vibrant, uniform colour, with creamy yellow fat. There should be small flecks of fat (marbling) throughout, as this helps the meat to be tender. Avoid meat with excess gristle. Bright red beef means that the animal has been butchered recently, whereas meat that has been hung in a traditional manner should be a deep, dark ruby red, almost purple. The darker the colour, especially with roasting joints, the more tender and succulent the beef will be.

~ Lamb Lamb is probably at its best in the spring, when the youngest lamb is available. It is tender to eat, with a delicate flavour, and its flesh is a paler pink than the older lamb, where the flesh is more red. The colour of the fat is also a good indication of age: young lamb fat is a very light, creamy colour. As the lamb matures, the fat becomes whiter and firmer. Imported lamb also has firmer, whiter fat. Lamb is naturally a fattier meat than beef, so take care when choosing. It used to be possible to buy mutton (lamb that is at least one year old), but this now tends to be available only in specialist outlets. It has a far stronger, almost gamey flavour and the joints tend to be larger.

∾ **Pork** Pork should be pale pink in colour and slightly marbled with small flecks of fat. There should be a layer of firm white fat with a thin elastic skin (rind), which can be scored before roasting to provide crackling. All cuts of pork are tender, as the pigs are slaughtered at an early age and are reared to be lean rather than fatty. Pork used to be well cooked, if not overcooked, due to the danger of the parasite trichina. This no longer applies, however, and it is now recommended that the meat is cooked less to keep it moist and tender.

∾ **Bacon, Gammon and Ham** Bacon and gammon are cured pork produced by injections of brine as well as immersion in brine or salt. The meat becomes a much paler pink with creamy white fat and rind. For smoked bacon, the meat is smoked after it is cured, which produces the darker brown rind and meat. Another name for unsmoked bacon is 'green' bacon, although this term is not used as much these days. Before cooking, it is often soaked in cold water in order to remove some of the salt. Cuts of bacon vary according to regions and in some areas, bacon is called ham.

Poultry

'Poultry' relates to turkey, chicken, poussin, duck and goose. It is low in saturated fat and is a good source of protein. Remove the skin before eating to keep it low-fat. Most is sold plucked, drawn and trussed.

Meat, Poultry & Fish

❧ Welfare Due to intensive farming used since the Second World War, chicken in particular offers a good source of cheap meat. However, there is a growing movement to return to the more traditional methods of farming, for better quality and better animal welfare. Free-range and organically grown chickens offer a far more succulent bird with excellent flavour, although they tend to be more expensive.

❧ Buying Both home-grown and imported poultry, fresh and frozen are available. When buying fresh poultry, look for plump birds with a flexible breast bone, and no unpleasant odour or green tinge. Frozen poultry should be rock hard with no ice crystals, as this could mean that the bird has thawed and been re-frozen. Avoid any produce where the packaging is damaged.

❧ Thawing and Storing When thawing, place in the refrigerator on a large plate and ensure that none of the juices drip onto other foods. Once thawed, remove all packaging, remove the giblets, if any, and reserve separately. Place on a plate and cover lightly. Use within 2 days. Treat fresh poultry the same way.

❧ Cooking Ensure that poultry is thoroughly cooked through and the juices run clear. Rest for 10 minutes before carving. Use within 2 days of cooking.

Fish and Seafood

Requiring only minimal cooking, all fish is an excellent choice for speedy and nutritious meals. There are two categories of fish: white and oily. The remaining types of seafood can be divided into three categories: shellfish, crustaceans and molluscs.

Buying and Storing Seafood Both types of fish are sold fresh or frozen as small whole fish, fillets or cutlets. Store as soon as possible in the refrigerator. Remove from the wrappings, place on a plate, cover lightly and store towards the top. Use within one day of purchase. If using frozen, thaw slowly in the refrigerator and use within one day of thawing.

Seafood should be eaten as fresh as possible. Live seafood gives the best flavour, as long as it is consumed on the day of purchase (and cleaned thoroughly). If live is not available, buy from a reputable source and eat on the day of purchase, refrigerating until required.

White Fish White fish such as cod, haddock, plaice or coley are an excellent source of protein and have a low fat content. They also contain vitamin B12 and niacin, plus important minerals such as phosphorous, iodine, selenium and potassium.

Oily Fish Oily fish such as sardines, mackerel, salmon and herring have a higher fat content than white fish, but are an excellent source of Omega-3 polyunsaturated fatty acids, important in fighting heart disease, cancers and arthritis. Oily fish also contain niacin, B6, B12 and D vitamins, and the minerals selenium, iodine, potassium and phosphorous. The taste is stronger and more robust, enabling stronger flavours such as chilli and garlic to be used. It is recommended that at least two portions of oily fish should be eaten each week.

Other Kinds of Seafood Shellfish include crustaceans, such as lobsters, which have hard shells that they shed and replace during their lifetime, and molluscs, which are animals that have hinged shells, such as scallops, or single shells, such as whelks. Other seafood includes cephalopods, such as squid, cuttlefish and octopus.

Meat, Poultry & Fish

Vegetables ❧ Salads

❦

Vegetables add colour, texture, flavour and valuable nutrients to a meal. They play an important role in the diet, providing necessary vitamins, minerals and fibre. Vegetables are versatile: they can be served as an accompaniment to other dishes – they go well with meat, poultry and fish – or they can be used as the basis for the whole meal.

Buying

When buying fresh vegetables, always look for ones that are bright and feel firm to the touch, and avoid any that are damaged or bruised. Choose onions and garlic that are hard and not sprouting; avoid ones that are soft, as they may be damaged. Salad leaves and other leaf vegetables should be fresh, bright and crisp – do not buy any that are wilted, look limp or have yellow leaves.

Storing

Many vegetables can be kept in a cool, dry, dark place, but some should be refrigerated.

- **Root vegetables, tubers and winter squashes** These should be kept in a cool, dry, dark place that is free of frost, such as a larder or garage. Winter squashes can be kept for several months if stored correctly.

- **Green vegetables, fruit vegetables and salad leaves** These should be kept in the salad drawer of the refrigerator.

∾ **Vegetables such as peas and beans** These do not keep for very long, so try to eat them as soon as possible after buying or picking.

Preparing

Always clean vegetables thoroughly before using. Brush or scrape off any dirt and wash well in cold water. Prepare the vegetables just before cooking, as once peeled, they lose nutrients. Do not leave them in water, as valuable water-soluble vitamins will be lost.

∾ **Lettuce and other salad** Wash leaves gently under cold running water and pull off and discard any tough stalks or outer leaves. Tear rather than cut the leaves. Dry thoroughly in a salad spinner or on paper towels before use, otherwise the leaves tend to wilt.

∾ **Spinach** This should be washed thoroughly to remove all traces of dirt. Cut off and discard any tough stalks and damaged leaves.

∾ **Leeks** These need to be thoroughly cleaned before use to remove any grit and dirt. After trimming the root and tough ends, make one cut lengthways (but not all the way along if you are intending to cook whole), and rinse under running water, getting right between the leaves.

∾ **Mushrooms** Since mushrooms have a high water content, it is generally advised not to wash them, in order to avoid them absorbing even more water. Therefore, most mushrooms can just be wiped with paper towels or a damp cloth.

Vegetables & Salad

Cooking Techniques

Vegetables can be cooked in a variety of different ways, such as baking, barbecuing, blanching, boiling, braising, deep-frying, grilling, roasting, sautéing, steaming and stir-frying.

∾ **Boiling** Always cook vegetables in a minimum amount of water and do not overcook, or valuable nutrients will be lost. It is best to cut vegetables into even-sized pieces and cook them briefly.

∾ **Blanching and Parboiling** These mean lightly cooking raw vegetables for a brief period of time, whether parboiling potatoes before roasting (see pages 50–51), cooking cabbage before braising or cooking leaf vegetables such as spinach. Spinach should be cooked in only the water clinging to its leaves for 2–3 minutes until wilted. Blanching is also used to remove skins easily from tomatoes. Cut a small cross in the top of the tomato and place in a heatproof bowl. Cover with boiling water and leave for a few seconds, then drain and peel off the skin.

∾ **Braising** This method is a slow way of cooking certain vegetables, notably red or white cabbage. The vegetable is simmered for a long period of time in a small amount of stock or water.

∾ **Steaming** This is a great way to cook vegetables such as broccoli, cauliflower, beans, carrots, parsnips and peas.

1. Cut the vegetables into even-sized pieces. Fill a large saucepan with about 5 cm/2 inches water, bring to the boil, then reduce to a simmer.

2. Place the vegetables in a metal steamer basket or colander and lower into the saucepan, then cover and steam until tender. Alternatively, use a plate standing on a trivet in the pan. Asparagus is traditionally cooked in an asparagus steamer. Do not let the water boil – it should just simmer.

3. Once tender, serve – there is no need to drain!

Microwaving Vegetables can be cooked very successfully in the microwave and they retain all their flavour and nutrients as well as their colour.

1. Prepare the vegetables, cutting into even-sized pieces. Place in a microwaveable bowl or arrange in a shallow dish.

2. For firm vegetables such as root vegetables, add 1–3 tablespoons water and cover with clingfilm. Pierce in a couple of places. Cook on high for 2–4 minutes, depending on how many vegetables and which variety are being cooked. The more delicate vegetables will require less cooking time and less water. Refer to manufacturer's guidelines to be sure of times.

3. Remove from the oven and leave to stand for 1–2 minutes before serving. Do not season until after cooking, especially with salt, as this will toughen the vegetables.

Grilling To grill peppers, cut in half or quarters and discard the seeds. Place, skin side uppermost on a foil-lined rack. Brush lightly with a little oil, then cook under the preheated grill for 5 minutes. Turn over, brush again and continue to grill for a further 3 minutes or until tender. Serve.

To grill aubergines, trim and wash, then cut into slices or lengths. Brush lightly with a little oil and place on a foil-lined grill rack. Cook under the preheated grill for 3–5 minutes or until the aubergine has softened. Turn over, brush again and grill for a further 3 minutes or until tender.

To grill tomatoes, rinse and cut in half. Place on a foil-lined grill rack and, if liked, season to taste. Cook under a preheated grill and cook for 3–5 minutes until cooked to personal preference.

Vegetables & Salad

∾ Grilling to Remove Skin To remove the skins from peppers:

1. Cut in half lengthways and deseed. Place skin-side up on the grill rack under a preheated hot grill and cook until the skins are blackened.

2. Remove with tongs and place in a polythene bag. Seal and leave for 8–10 minutes, until the peppers are cool enough to handle.

3. Once cool, remove from the bag and carefully peel away the blackened skin.

∾ Stir-frying Stir-frying is an excellent way of serving all manner of vegetables. This way, all the nutrients are retained due to the short cooking time. Vegetables suitable for stir-frying are: peppers, courgettes, sugar snap peas, beans, baby corn, carrots, pak choi, spinach, tiny broccoli florets, spring onions and mushrooms, as well as sprouting seeds and shoots. To stir-fry:

1. Prepare all the vegetables before starting to cook. Peel, trim then cut any large pieces of vegetables into thin strips.

2. Heat a wok or frying pan for 1 minute or until very hot, then add 1–2 tablespoons oil and carefully swirl the pan with the hot oil.

3. Add spices and flavours such as grated root ginger, chopped chilli and lemon grass and cook for 1 minute, then add the prepared vegetables, starting with the firmest, such as carrot.

4. Using a large spatula or spoon, stir-fry over a high heat, adding soy or other sauce as required. Cook for about 3–4 minutes, ensuring that the vegetables are still crisp.

∾ Sweating This method cooks vegetables such as onions in their own juices with or without a little oil. The vegetables should not be browned by this method and will retain masses of flavour and nutrients.

1. Prepare and clean the vegetables and cut into even-sized pieces.

2. Place in a frying pan or large saucepan over a low heat, with a little oil, if liked.

3. Cover with a lid and cook very gently in the steam that is generated. Stir occasionally. Use either in a casserole or as the basis for a soup or sauce.

❧ Frying This method relates to cooking vegetables in oil. It can be either shallow frying or deep frying (*see* also page 48 for sautéing). Shallow frying uses a minimal amount of oil whereas with deep frying the vegetables are plunged into hot oil.

To shallow fry:

1. Prepare the vegetables and cut into even-sized pieces. Heat some oil in a frying pan and add the vegetables.

2. Fry over a medium heat for 12–15 minutes until cooked and golden.

To deep fry:

1. Prepare the vegetables and cut into even sized pieces. Half fill a deep fryer, large saucepan or wok with oil such as sunflower or vegetable oil. Heat to 180°C/350°F or when a small cube of bread turns golden in 30 seconds.

2. Place the food to be fried in the frying basket or on a wide, flat slotted spoon and carefully lower into the hot oil. Take care if the food is slightly wet as it may spit.

3. Cook for 5–10 minutes until the food is golden and cooked. Drain on kitchen paper and serve.

❧ Roasting Suitable for vegetables such as fennel, courgettes, pumpkin, squash, peppers, garlic, aubergines, potatoes, onions and tomatoes. Cut the vegetables into even-sized chunks. Heat some oil in a roasting tin in a preheated oven at 200°C/400°F/Gas Mark 6. Put the vegetables in the hot oil, baste and roast in the oven for 30 minutes. Garlic can be split into different cloves or whole heads can be roasted. It is best not to peel them until cooked.

Vegetables & Salad

Soups &

Small Meals

Soup is probably one of the simplest things to make as a student. It can be healthy and hearty, you can add anything you like, and it stores well too. From Bacon & Split Pea to Winter Hotchpot, this chapter offers a great selection of soups for you to try. Or if you are looking for a light lunch, or something to use as a side-dish, the small meals in this chapter are just perfect, you are sure to love the deliciously crispy Potato Skins or the Chicken Wraps.

Pumpkin Soup

Makes 1 portion

175 g/6 oz pumpkin flesh (after
peeling and discarding the seeds),
cut into 2.5 cm/1 inch cubes
1 tbsp olive or sunflower oil
1 small onion, peeled
1 small leek, trimmed
1 small carrot, peeled
1 small celery stalk
1 garlic clove, peeled and crushed
450 ml/³/₄ pint water
salt and freshly ground
black pepper
freshly grated nutmeg, to taste
2 tbsp milk
cayenne pepper, to taste (optional)
1 tbsp single cream (optional)
warm herby bread, to serve

Heat the oil in a large saucepan and cook the pumpkin for 2–3 minutes, coating it in the oil. Chop the onion and leek finely and cut the carrot and celery into small dice. Add the vegetables to the saucepan with the garlic and cook, stirring, for 5 minutes or until they have begun to soften. Cover with the water and bring to the boil. Season with plenty of salt and pepper and the nutmeg, cover and simmer for 15–20 minutes until all of the vegetables are tender.

Remove from the heat, cool slightly then blend to a smooth purée using a handheld blender (or a food processor or liquidizer if you have one). Pass through a sieve into a clean saucepan. Adjust the seasoning to taste and add the milk with sufficient water to obtain the correct consistency. Bring the soup to boiling point, add the cayenne pepper, if using, and serve immediately swirled with the cream, if using, with warm herby bread.

Store any remaining soup, when cool, in the fridge in a bowl covered with clingfilm or pour into a small freezer bag placed in a wide-mouth jar and freeze for 4 hours or until solid. Remove from the jar and secure the bag, label and date. Use within 1 month. The soup is easily thawed: simply place the bag in the saucepan you will use for reheating and leave for about 6 hours or overnight. To reheat, tip the contents of the bag into the pan and heat over a gentle heat, stirring frequently. Add a little extra milk if too thick. Heat until piping hot.

Curried Parsnip Soup

Makes 1 portion

1 tsp olive or sunflower oil
1 small onion, peeled and chopped
1 garlic clove, peeled and crushed
$^1/_2$–1 tsp medium/hot curry powder
1 cinnamon stick (optional)
175 g/6 oz parsnips, peeled
and chopped
450 ml/$^3/_4$ pint vegetable stock
salt and freshly ground black pepper
1 tbsp low-fat natural yogurt, to serve
fresh coriander leaves,
to garnish (optional)

Heat the oil in a saucepan. Cook the onion until softened and starting to turn golden.

Add the garlic, curry powder to taste and cinnamon stick, if using, to the pan. Continue to cook for a further 2 minutes, stirring frequently.

Add the parsnips and stir well. Pour in the stock and bring to the boil. Cover and simmer for 15 minutes or until the parsnips are cooked.

Allow the soup to cool. Once cooled, remove the cinnamon stick, if used, and discard.

Blend the soup with a handheld blender until very smooth. Reheat gently. Season to taste with salt and pepper. Garnish with fresh coriander, if using, and serve immediately with the yogurt.

Store any remaining soup, when cool, in the fridge in a bowl covered with clingfilm or pour into a small freezer bag placed in a wide-mouth jar and freeze for 4 hours or until solid. Remove from the jar and secure the bag, label and date. Use within 1 month (*see* page 64 for reheating instructions).

Carrot & Ginger Soup

Makes 1 portion

1–2 slices of bread, crusts removed (optional)
1 tsp yeast extract (optional)
2 tsp olive oil
1 small onion, peeled and chopped
1 garlic clove, peeled and crushed
$1/2$–1 tsp ground ginger
225 g/8 oz carrots, peeled and chopped
450 ml/³/₄ pint vegetable stock
2.5 cm/1 inch piece of root ginger, peeled and finely grated or an extra 1 tsp ground ginger
salt and freshly ground black pepper
1 tbsp lemon juice

To garnish:

chives (optional)
lemon zest (optional)

If making the croutons, preheat the oven to 180°C/350°F/Gas Mark 4. Roughly chop the bread. Dissolve the yeast extract in 2 tablespoons of warm water and mix with the bread. Spread the bread cubes over a lightly oiled baking tray and bake for 20 minutes, turning halfway through. Remove from the oven and reserve.

Heat the oil in a large saucepan. Gently cook the onion and garlic for 3–4 minutes. Stir in the ground ginger and cook for 1 minute to release the flavour. Add the chopped carrots, then stir in the stock and the fresh ginger, if using. Simmer gently for 15 minutes.

Remove from the heat and allow to cool a little. Blend until smooth, then season to taste with salt and pepper. Stir in the lemon juice. Garnish with the croutons, chives and lemon zest, if using, and serve immediately.

If wishing to keep the soup for the next day, pour into a bowl, cover with clingfilm and store when cool in the fridge. Reheat gently stirring frequently until piping hot.

Swede, Turnip, Parsnip & Potato Soup

Makes 1 portion

1 medium onion, peeled
2 tsp butter or margarine
1 small carrot, peeled and
roughly chopped
75 g/3 oz swede, peeled and
roughly chopped
1 small turnip, peeled and
roughly chopped
1 small parsnip, peeled and
roughly chopped
1 medium potato, peeled
450 ml/³/₄ pint vegetable stock
¹/₂ tsp freshly grated nutmeg
(optional)
salt and freshly ground
black pepper
1 tbsp vegetable oil, for frying
50 ml/2 fl oz milk
warm crusty bread, to serve

Finely slice the onion. Melt the butter or margarine in a medium saucepan and add half the onion with the carrot, swede, turnip, parsnip and potato. Cover and cook very gently for about 10 minutes, without colouring. Stir occasionally during this time. Add the stock and season to taste with the nutmeg, if using, and salt and pepper. Cover and bring to the boil, then reduce the heat and simmer gently for 15–20 minutes, or until the vegetables are tender. Remove from the heat and leave to cool for 30 minutes.

Heat the oil in a heavy-based frying pan. Add the remaining onion and cook over a medium heat, for about 2–3 minutes, stirring frequently, until golden brown. Remove the onion with a slotted spoon and drain well on absorbent kitchen paper. As it cools, it will turn crispy.

Pour the cooled soup into a food processor, or use a handheld blender, and process to form a smooth purée. Return to the cleaned pan, adjust the seasoning, then stir in the milk. Gently reheat and top with the crispy onions. Serve immediately with chunks of bread.

Store any remaining soup, when cool, in the fridge in a bowl covered with clingfilm or pour into a small freezer bag placed in a wide-mouth jar and freezer for 4 hours or until solid. Remove from the jar and secure the bag, label and date. Use within 1 month (*see* page 64 for reheating instructions).

Potato, Leek & Rosemary Soup

Makes 1 portion

1 tbsp butter or margarine
1 leek, trimmed and finely sliced
1 medium potato, peeled and
roughly chopped
300 ml/^{1}/$_2$ vegetable stock
1 fresh rosemary sprig
150 ml/^{1}/$_4$ pint milk
1 tsp freshly chopped parsley
1 tsp crème fraîche (optional)
salt and freshly ground
black pepper
wholemeal rolls, to serve

Melt the butter or margarine in a medium saucepan, add the leek and cook gently for 5 minutes, stirring frequently. If liked, remove 1 tablespoon of the cooked leeks and reserve for garnishing.

Add the potato, vegetable stock, rosemary sprig and milk. Bring to the boil, then reduce the heat, cover and simmer gently for 20–25 minutes, or until the vegetables are tender.

Cool for 10 minutes. Discard the rosemary, then pour into a food processor or use a handheld blender and blend well to form a smooth-textured soup.

Return the soup to the cleaned saucepan and stir in the chopped parsley and crème fraîche, if using. Season to taste with salt and pepper. If the soup is too thick, stir in a little more milk or water. Reheat gently without boiling, then ladle into a warm soup bowl. Garnish the soup with the reserved leeks and serve immediately with wholemeal rolls.

Store any remaining soup, when cool, in the fridge in a bowl covered with clingfilm or pour into a small freezer bag placed in a wide-mouth jar and freezer for 4 hours or until solid. Remove from the jar and secure the bag, label and date. Use within 1 month (*see* page 64 for reheating instructions).

Italian Bean Soup

Makes 1 portion

2 tsp olive or sunflower oil
1 small leek, washed and chopped
1 garlic clove, peeled and crushed
1 tsp dried oregano
25 g/1 oz green beans, trimmed
and cut into bite-size pieces
50 g/2 oz canned cannellini beans,
drained and rinsed (or 25 g/1 oz
dried beans if preferred)
40 g/1^{1}/$_{2}$ oz small pasta shapes
450 ml/^{3}/$_{4}$ pint vegetable stock
4 cherry tomatoes
salt and freshly ground
black pepper
freshly shredded basil leaves
(optional)

If using dried beans, soak them overnight in a bowl covered with water. The next day, rinse then place in a saucepan and cover with fresh water. Bring to the boil, reduce to a gentle boil and cook for 10 minutes. Drain, rinse and return to the pan. Cover with cold water, bring to the boil, reduce to a simmer and cook covered with a lid for 1–1^{1}/$_{2}$ hours or until tender. Drain and use as required.

Heat the oil in a medium saucepan. Add the leek, garlic and oregano and cook gently for 5 minutes, stirring occasionally. Stir in the green beans and the cannellini beans. Sprinkle in the pasta and pour in the stock. Bring the stock mixture to the boil, then reduce the heat to a simmer. Cook for 12–15 minutes or until the vegetables are tender and the pasta is cooked to *al dente*. Stir occasionally.

In a heavy-based frying pan, dry-fry the tomatoes over a high heat until they soften and begin to blacken. Gently crush the tomatoes in the pan with the back of a spoon and add to the soup. Season to taste with salt and pepper. Stir in the shredded basil and serve immediately.

Store any remaining soup, when cool, in the fridge in a bowl covered with clingfilm and use within 3 days. This soup will freeze, but add more basil when reheating.

Rice & Tomato Soup

Makes 1 portion

25 g/1 oz easy-cook basmati rice
2 canned tomatoes
plus 1 tbsp of juice
1 garlic clove, peeled and crushed
1 tsp grated lemon or lime zest
1 tsp olive or sunflower oil
pinch sugar
salt and freshly ground
black pepper
300 ml/^{1}/$_2$ pint vegetable stock
or water, boiling

For the croutons:

2 tsp ready-made pesto sauce
2 tsp olive or sunflower oil
2 slices ciabatta bread, cut into
1 cm/^{1}/$_2$ inch cubes

Preheat the oven to 220°C/425°F/Gas Mark 7. Rinse and drain the basmati rice. Chop the canned tomatoes and place with their juice in a medium heavy-based saucepan with the garlic, lime or lemon zest, oil and sugar. Season to taste with salt and pepper. Bring to the boil, then reduce the heat, cover and simmer for 10 minutes.

Add the boiling vegetable stock or water and the rice, then cook, uncovered, for a further 15–20 minutes, or until the rice is tender. If the soup is too thick, add a little more water. Reserve and keep warm, if the croutons are not ready.

Meanwhile, to make the croutons, mix the pesto and oil in a bowl. Add the bread cubes and toss until they are coated completely with the mixture. Spread on a baking sheet and bake in the preheated oven for 10–15 minutes, until golden and crisp, turning them over halfway through cooking. Serve the soup immediately sprinkled with the warm croutons.

Store any remaining soup, when cool, in the fridge in a bowl covered with clingfilm and use within 1–2 days. Do not freeze.

Bacon & Split Pea Soup

Makes 1 portion

25 g/1 oz dried split peas
1 tsp butter or margarine
1 garlic clove, peeled and
finely chopped
1 small onion, peeled
and thinly sliced
25 g/1 oz long-grain rice
1–2 tsp tomato purée
450 ml/³/₄ pint vegetable
or chicken stock
1 small carrot, peeled and
finely diced
2–3 rashers streaky bacon,
finely chopped
salt and freshly ground
black pepper
1 tsp freshly chopped parsley
1 tbsp single cream or milk
warm crusty garlic bread, to serve

Cover the dried split peas with plenty of cold water, cover loosely and leave to soak for a minimum of 12 hours, preferably overnight.

Melt the butter or margarine in a heavy-based saucepan, add the garlic and onion and cook for 2–3 minutes, without colouring. Add the rice, drained split peas and tomato purée and cook for 2–3 minutes, stirring constantly to prevent sticking. Add the stock, bring to the boil, then reduce the heat and simmer for 20–25 minutes until the rice and peas are tender. Remove from the heat and leave to cool. Blend about three-quarters of the soup in a separate bowl with a handheld blender to form a smooth purée. Pour the purée into the remaining soup in the pan. Add the carrot and cook for a further 10–12 minutes, or until the carrot is tender.

Meanwhile, place the bacon in a nonstick frying pan and cook over a gentle heat until the bacon is crisp. Remove and drain on kitchen paper. Season the soup with salt and pepper to taste, then stir in the parsley and milk or cream. Reheat for 2–3 minutes, then ladle into soup bowls. Sprinkle with the bacon and serve immediately with warm garlic bread.

This soup keeps well so why not double up and make enough for 2–3 days. Keep covered in the refrigerator. It is not so suitable for freezing. When reheating, make sure that the soup is brought to the boil then simmered for at least 10 minutes – it needs to be piping hot before eating.

Bread & Tomato Soup

Makes 1 portion

225 g/8 oz very ripe tomatoes
1 tbsp olive or sunflower oil
1 small onion, peeled and
finely chopped
2–3 freshly chopped basil leaves
1 garlic clove, peeled and crushed
$^1/_4$ tsp hot chilli powder
salt and freshly ground
black pepper
300 ml/$^1/_2$ pint chicken stock
2–3 slices stale white bread
1 tbsp cucumber, cut into
small dice
whole basil leaves,
to garnish (optional)

Make a small cross in the base of each tomato, then place in a bowl and cover with boiling water. Allow to stand for 2 minutes, or until the skins have started to peel away, then drain, remove the skins and seeds and chop into large pieces.

Heat the olive oil in a saucepan and gently cook the onion until softened. Add the skinned tomatoes, chopped basil, garlic and chilli powder and season to taste with salt and pepper. Pour in the stock, cover the saucepan, bring to the boil and simmer gently for 15–20 minutes.

Remove the crusts from the bread and break into small pieces. Remove the tomato mixture from the heat and stir in the bread. Cover and leave to stand for 10 minutes, or until the bread has blended with the tomatoes. Season to taste. Serve warm or cold, garnished with a spoonful of chopped cucumber and basil leaves, if using.

This soup will thicken if kept overnight. Store in the refrigerator, lightly covered with clingfilm. If too thick when required, simply thin down a little with stock or water. This soup will not be so good if frozen.

Chinese Chicken Soup

Makes 1 portion

50 g/2 oz cooked chicken
1 tsp groundnut or olive oil
2 spring onions, trimmed and
diagonally sliced
$1/2$–1 red chilli, deseeded and
finely chopped
1 garlic clove, peeled and crushed
1.25 cm/$1/2$ inch piece root ginger,
peeled and finely grated
450 ml/$3/4$ pint chicken stock
50 g/2 oz medium egg noodles
1 small carrot, peeled and cut
into matchsticks
25 g/1 oz beansprouts
2 tsp soy sauce
1 tsp fish sauce (optional)
fresh coriander leaves, to garnish
(optional)

Remove any skin or bones from the chicken. Place on a chopping board and use two forks to tear the chicken into fine shreds.

Heat the oil in a medium saucepan and fry the spring onions and chilli for 1 minute. Add the garlic and ginger and cook for another minute.

Stir in the chicken stock and gradually bring the mixture to the boil.

Break up the noodles a little and add to the boiling stock with the carrot.

Stir to mix, then reduce the heat to a simmer and cook for 3–4 minutes.

Add the shredded chicken, beansprouts, soy sauce and fish sauce, if using, and stir.

Cook for a further 2–3 minutes until piping hot. Ladle the soup into bowls and sprinkle with the coriander leaves, if using. Serve immediately.

This soup will not keep that well, so eat up!

Winter Hotchpot

Makes 1 portion

small piece gammon, about
125 g/4 oz, or use bacon rashers
1 tsp olive oil
1 small onion, peeled and
finely chopped
1 garlic clove, peeled and
finely chopped
1 medium carrot, peeled
and finely chopped
1 celery stalk, trimmed
and finely sliced
1 leek, trimmed and finely sliced
450 ml/³/₄ pint ham or vegetable stock
25 g/1 oz pearl barley, rinsed
freshly ground black pepper
crusty bread, to serve

Remove any rind and fat from the gammon or bacon rashers and cut into small pieces.

Heat the oil in a medium saucepan over a medium heat and add all the prepared vegetables and gammon or bacon. Cook, stirring occasionally, for 5–8 minutes until the vegetables have softened.

Pour in the stock and bring to the boil. Cover with a lid and simmer for 10 minutes. Add the pearl barley to the pan.

Continue to simmer, covered, for 15–20 minutes until the vegetables and gammon are tender. Add freshly ground black pepper to taste, then serve with crusty bread.

This soup will not freeze well but any remaining soup will keep in the fridge in a clean bowl covered with clingfilm for up to 2 days. Thin down with extra stock or water if too thick after keeping.

Potato Skins

Makes 4 Portions

4 large baking potatoes
2 tbsp olive oil
2 tsp paprika
125 g/4 oz unsmoked streaky bacon
rashers, roughly chopped
6 tbsp milk
125 g/4 oz Gorgonzola or Stilton cheese
1 tbsp freshly chopped parsley

To serve:

reduced-calorie mayonnaise
sweet chilli dipping sauce
tossed green salad

Preheat the oven to 200°C/400°F/Gas Mark 6. Scrub the potatoes, then prick a few times with a fork or skewer and place directly on the top shelf of the oven. Bake in the preheated oven for at least 1 hour, or until tender. The potatoes are cooked when they yield gently to the pressure of your hand. Set the potatoes aside until cool enough to handle, then cut in half and scoop the flesh into a bowl and reserve.

Preheat the grill and line the grill rack with tinfoil. Mix together the oil and the paprika and use half to brush the outside of the potato skins. Place on the grill rack under the preheated hot grill and cook for 5 minutes, or until crisp, turning as necessary. Heat the remaining paprika-flavoured oil and gently fry the bacon until crisp. Add to the potato flesh along with the milk, cheese and parsley. Halve the potato skins and fill with the cheese filling. Return to the oven for a further 15 minutes to heat through. Sprinkle with a little more paprika and serve immediately with mayonnaise, sweet chilli sauce and a green salad.

Only do the last 15 minutes in the oven for the potatoes that you will eat now. Place the remaining potatoes on a plate, cover with clingfilm and store in the refrigerator for 2–3 days. Cook at the above temperature for 20 minutes or until piping hot. Or, you can microwave the raw potatoes for 4–6 minutes each. Finish as per the recipe. To reheat, place on a plate, cover with clingfilm, pierce a couple of times, then heat on High for 1 minute for each potato. Allow to stand for 1 minute before eating.

Chinese Fried Rice

Makes 1 portion

125 g/4 oz long-grain rice
2 tsp groundnut or vegetable oil
1–2 bacon rashers, chopped
1 garlic clove, peeled and
finely chopped
1 tsp freshly grated root ginger
1 tbsp frozen peas, thawed
1 medium egg, beaten
25 g/1 oz beansprouts
salt and freshly ground
black pepper

To garnish:

1 tbsp roasted peanuts, chopped
1 spring onion, trimmed

Wash the rice in several changes of water until it runs relatively clear. Drain well. Put into a saucepan or flameproof casserole dish with a tight-fitting lid. Pour in enough water to cover the rice by about 1 cm/$\frac{1}{2}$ inch. Add salt and bring to the boil. As soon as the water boils, cover the saucepan, reduce the heat as low as possible and cook for 10 minutes. Remove from the heat and leave to stand for a further 10 minutes. Do not lift the lid while cooking. Leave until cold, and then stir with a fork.

Heat a wok or frying pan, add the oil and, when hot, add the chopped bacon. Stir-fry for 1 minute before adding the garlic and ginger, then stir-fry for a further 30 seconds. Add the cooked rice and peas to the wok or frying pan. Stir-fry over a high heat for 5 minutes. Add the egg and the beansprouts and continue to stir-fry for a further 2 minutes until the egg has set. Season to taste with salt and pepper. Spoon the mixture onto a serving plate and garnish with the peanuts and spring onions. Serve hot or cold.

Spoon any remaining rice into a bowl, cover with clingfilm and store in the refrigerator for the next day. If reheating, ensure that the rice is piping hot before eating. Delicious eaten cold with an omelette. I would not recommend freezing this dish.

Mediterranean Feast

Makes 2 portions

3–4 lettuce leaves such as round cos
50 g/2 oz French beans
75 g/3 oz new potatoes, scrubbed
2 medium eggs
1 small green pepper
1 small onion, peeled
125 g/4 oz canned tuna in brine,
drained and flaked into small pieces
1–2 tbsp low-fat hard cheese, such
as Edam, cut into small cubes
8 ripe but firm cherry tomatoes,
quartered
25 g/1 oz black pitted olives,
halved (optional)
freshly chopped basil, to garnish

For the vinaigrette:

2 tbsp light olive or vegetable oil
1 tbsp each white wine vinegar,
lemon juice and grated lemon zest
1 tsp Dijon mustard
1 tsp caster sugar, or to taste
salt and freshly ground black pepper

Tear the lettuce into bite-sized pieces and arrange on a serving platter or two individual plates. Cook the French beans in boiling salted water for 8 minutes and the potatoes for 10 minutes or until tender. Drain and rinse in cold water until cool, then cut both the beans and potatoes in half with a sharp knife. Boil the eggs for 10 minutes, then rinse thoroughly under a cold running tap until cool. Remove the shells under water and cut each egg into quarters. Remove the seeds from the pepper and cut into thin strips and finely chop the onion. Arrange the beans, potatoes, eggs, peppers and onion on top of the lettuce. Add the tuna, cheese and tomatoes. Sprinkle over the olives, if using, and garnish with the basil.

To make the vinaigrette, place all the ingredients in a screw-topped jar and shake vigorously until everything is mixed thoroughly. Spoon 2 tablespoons over the top of the prepared salad and serve the remainder separately.

If wishing to share this meal with a friend or to keep some for the next day, do not pour the dressing over but serve separately. Store the salad in a bowl, covered with clingfilm in the refrigerator.

Sweetcorn Fritters

Makes 2 portions

3 tbsp vegetable oil
1 small onion, peeled and finely chopped
$^1/_2$–1 red chilli, deseeded and finely chopped
1 garlic clove, peeled and crushed
$^1/_2$ tsp ground coriander
175 g/6 oz canned or thawed frozen sweetcorn
2 spring onions, trimmed and finely sliced
1 egg, lightly beaten
salt and freshly ground black pepper
1–2 tbsp plain flour
$^1/_2$ tsp baking powder
spring onion curls, to garnish (optional)
Thai-style chutney, to serve

Heat 1 tablespoon of the oil in a frying pan, add the onion and cook gently for 7–8 minutes or until beginning to soften. Add the chilli, garlic and ground coriander and cook for 1 minute, stirring continuously. Remove from the heat.

Drain the sweetcorn and tip into a mixing bowl. Lightly mash with a potato masher to break down the corn a little. Add the cooked onion mixture to the bowl with the spring onions and beaten egg. Season to taste with salt and pepper, and then stir to mix together. Sift the flour and baking powder over the mixture and stir in. Heat 2 tablespoons of the oil in a large frying pan. Drop 4 or 5 heaped teaspoonfuls of the sweetcorn mixture into the pan, and using a fish slice or spatula, flatten each to make a 1 cm/$^1/_2$ inch thick fritter. Fry the fritters for 3 minutes, or until golden brown on the underside, turn over and fry for a further 3 minutes, or until cooked through and crisp. Remove the fritters from the pan and drain on absorbent kitchen paper. Keep warm while cooking the remaining fritters, adding a little more oil if needed. Garnish with spring onion curls, if using, and serve immediately with a Thai-style chutney.

If any fritters remain uneaten, store on a plate lightly covered in the refrigerator overnight. Fry in a little oil on both sides to reheat. Take care not to burn but ensure that the fritters are piping hot. Drain on kitchen paper to absorb any excess oil.

Spanish Omelette with Fish

Makes 1 portion

2 tbsp sunflower oil
125 g/4 oz potatoes, peeled and
cut into 1 cm/$\frac{1}{2}$ inch cubes
1 small onion, peeled
and cut into wedges
1 large garlic clove,
peeled and thinly sliced
1 small red pepper, deseeded,
quartered and thinly sliced
50 g/2 oz fresh white fish such
as coley or whiting
salt and freshly ground black pepper
1 tbsp butter or margarine, melted
1 tbsp milk
2 medium eggs, beaten
2 tsp freshly chopped
flat-leaf parsley
2 tbsp mature Cheddar
cheese, grated

To serve:
crusty bread
tossed green salad, to serve

Heat the oil in a medium nonstick heavy-based frying pan, add the potatoes, onion and garlic and cook gently for 10–15 minutes until golden brown, then add the red pepper and cook for 3 minutes.

Discard any skin or small bones from the fish. Cut into small pieces. Place into a bowl, toss in the melted butter or margarine with the milk and add seasoning. Reserve.

When the vegetables are cooked, drain off any excess oil and stir in the beaten egg with the chopped parsley. Pour the fish mixture over the top and cook gently for 5 minutes, or until the eggs become firm.

Sprinkle the grated cheese over the top and place the pan under a preheated hot grill. Cook for 2–3 minutes until the cheese is golden and bubbling. Carefully slide the omelette onto a large plate and serve immediately with plenty of bread and salad.

Chicken Wraps

Makes 2 portions

For the stir-fried chicken:

2 skinless chicken breast fillets
finely grated zest and juice
of 1 lemon
2 tsp sugar
1–2 tsp dried oregano
$^1\!/_2$ tsp ground cinnamon
$^1\!/_4$ tsp cayenne pepper or to taste
$1^1\!/_2$ tbsp sunflower oil
1 small onion, peeled and sliced
1 small green, red and yellow pepper,
deseeded and sliced
salt and freshly ground black pepper

To serve:

flour tortillas
sour cream
guacamole

Slice the chicken across the grain into strips. Place in a bowl with the lemon zest and juice, sugar, oregano, cinnamon and cayenne pepper. Mix well and leave to marinate in the refrigerator for at least 30 minutes, or longer if time permits.

Heat $^1\!/_2$ tablespoon of the oil in a wok or frying pan and stir-fry the onion for 5 minutes until lightly coloured. Remove with a slotted spoon and reserve.

When ready to eat, heat 2–4 tortillas as directed on the packet. Keep warm.

Add the remaining oil to the wok or frying pan and heat. Drain the chicken from the marinade and add it to pan. Cook for 8 minutes, then return the onions, add the pepper slices and cook for a further 4–5 minutes, or until the chicken is cooked through and the vegetables are tender. Season to taste with salt and pepper and serve immediately with the warm tortillas, sour cream and guacamole.

Any remaining chicken and vegetable mix will keep well in the refrigerator. Once cool, place on a plate, cover with clingfilm and keep overnight in the refrigerator. Use cold the next day, in a warmed tortilla.

Smoked Haddock Rösti

Makes 1 portion

125 g/4 oz potatoes, peeled and
coarsely grated
1 small onion, peeled and
coarsely grated
1 garlic clove, peeled
and crushed
75 g/3 oz smoked haddock,
thawed if frozen
2 tsp olive or vegetable oil
salt and freshly ground black pepper
1 tsp finely grated lemon zest
1 tsp freshly chopped parsley
1 tbsp half-fat crème fraîche
or natural yoghurt
lemon wedges, to serve (optional)
mixed salad leaves, to garnish

Dry the grated potatoes in a clean tea towel. Rinse the grated onion thoroughly in cold water, dry in a clean tea towel and add to the potatoes. Stir the garlic into the potato mixture.

Skin the smoked haddock and remove as many of the tiny pin bones as possible. Cut into thin slices and reserve.

Heat the oil in a small non-stick frying pan. Add half the potatoes and press well down in the frying pan. Season to taste with salt and pepper. Add a layer of fish and a sprinkling of lemon zest, parsley and black pepper. Top with the remaining potatoes and press down firmly. Cover with a sheet of kitchen foil and cook on the lowest heat for 25–30 minutes.

Preheat the grill 2–3 minutes before the end of cooking time. Remove the kitchen foil and place the rosti under the grill to brown. Turn out on to a warmed serving dish, and serve immediately with spoonfuls of crème fraîche, lemon wedges and mixed salad leaves.

If you have any rösti left over, keep for the next day or freeze. If keeping, once cool, place on a plate, cover with clingfilm and leave overnight in the refrigerator. If freezing, allow to cool then wrap in kitchen foil, label, date and place in the freezer. Thaw in the refrigerator for at least 6–8 hours and reheat by heating 1 tbsp of oil in a pan then frying for 3–4 minutes on each side.

Turkey Hash with Potato & Beetroot

Makes 1 portion

2 tsp vegetable oil
15 g/¹/₂ oz butter or margarine
1 rasher streaky bacon, diced or sliced
1 small onion, peeled and finely chopped
125 g/4 oz cooked turkey, diced
125 g/4 oz finely chopped cooked potatoes
1 tsp freshly chopped parsley
2 tsp plain flour
75g/3 oz cooked beetroot, diced
green salad, to serve

In a small heavy-based frying pan, heat the oil and half the butter or margarine over a medium heat until sizzling. Add the bacon and cook for 2 minutes, or until crisp and golden, stirring occasionally. Using a slotted spoon, transfer to a bowl. Add the onion to the pan and cook for 3–4 minutes, or until soft and golden, stirring frequently.

Meanwhile, add the turkey, potatoes, parsley and flour to the cooked bacon in the bowl. Stir and toss gently, then fold in the diced beetroot.

Add half the remaining butter or margarine to the frying pan and then the turkey vegetable mixture. Stir, then spread the mixture to evenly cover the bottom of the frying pan. Cook over a medium heat for 15 minutes, or until the underside is crisp and brown, pressing the hash firmly into a cake with a spatula. Remove from the heat.

Invert a large plate over the frying pan and, holding the plate and frying pan together with an oven glove, turn the hash out onto the plate. Heat the remaining butter or margarine in the pan, slide the hash back into the pan and cook for 4 minutes, or until crisp and brown on the other side. Invert onto the plate again and serve immediately with a green salad.

Huevos Rancheros

Makes 1 portion

2 tsp olive or vegetable oil
1 small onion, peeled and
finely chopped
$1/2$ small red pepper, deseeded and
finely chopped
1 garlic clove, peeled and
finely chopped
1–2 green chillies, deseeded and
finely chopped, and/
or $1/2$ tsp chilli powder
$1/2$ tsp ground cumin
$1/2$ tsp ground coriander
1 tsp freshly chopped coriander
2 medium-sized ripe plum
tomatoes, peeled, deseeded
and roughly chopped
$1/4$ tsp sugar
2 small eggs
2 flour tortillas
salt and freshly ground black pepper
sprigs of fresh coriander, to garnish
refried beans, to serve (optional)

Heat the oil in a medium heavy-based saucepan. Add the onion and pepper and cook over a medium heat for 10 minutes. Add the garlic, chillies and/or chilli powder, ground cumin and ground and chopped coriander and cook for a further minute. Add the tomatoes and sugar. Stir well, cover and cook gently for 10 minutes. Uncover and cook for a further 8–10 minutes.

Lightly poach the eggs in a small frying pan, filled with gently simmering water. Drain well and keep warm.

Place the tortillas briefly under a preheated hot grill. Turn once and remove from the grill when hot.

Season the tomato sauce to taste with salt and pepper. To serve, arrange the tortillas on a serving plate, top with the two eggs and spoon the sauce over. Garnish with sprigs of fresh coriander and serve immediately with warmed refried beans, if liked.

The tomato sauce will keep well in the refrigerator. Spoon into a small bowl and cover with clingfilm. Use within 2–3 days.

Garlic Mushroom Galettes

Makes 2

50 g/2 oz piece bought puff pastry
1 small onion, peeled
1 red chilli, deseeded
2 garlic cloves, peeled
75 g/3 oz mixed mushrooms (e.g.
large field, button or chestnut)
25 g/1 oz butter or margarine
1 tsp freshly chopped parsley
50 g/2 oz mozzarella
cheese, sliced

To serve:

cherry tomatoes
mixed green salad leaves

Preheat the oven to 220°C/425°F/Gas Mark 7. On a lightly floured surface roll out the pastry very thinly. Cut out two 15 cm/6 inch circles and place on a lightly oiled baking sheet.

Slice the onion thinly, then divide into rings and reserve. Slice the chilli thinly and slice the garlic into wafer-thin slivers. Add to the onions and reserve. Wipe or lightly rinse the mushrooms. Halve or quarter any large mushrooms and keep the small ones whole.

Heat the butter or margarine in a frying pan and fry the onion, chilli and garlic gently for about 3 minutes. Add the mushrooms and cook for about 5 minutes, or until beginning to soften. Stir the parsley into the mushroom mixture and drain off any excess liquid.

Pile the mushroom mixture onto the pastry circles within 5 mm/$1/4$ inch of the edge. Arrange the sliced mozzarella cheese on top. Bake in the preheated oven for 12–15 minutes, or until golden brown and serve with the tomatoes and salad.

If you only want to make one galette for now, cook one then place the remaining filling in a small bowl, and the spare pastry round on a clean baking tray, cover and store both overnight in the refrigerator. Cook the next evening.

Spanish Baked Tomatoes

Makes 1–2 portions

50 g/2 oz whole-grain rice
300 ml/¹/₂ pint vegetable stock
2 tsp sunflower oil
1 shallot, peeled and finely chopped
1 garlic clove, peeled and crushed
¹/₂ green pepper, deseeded and cut into small dice
¹/₂–1 red chilli, deseeded and finely chopped
25 g/1 oz button mushrooms finely chopped
1 tsp freshly chopped oregano
salt and freshly ground black pepper
2 large ripe beef tomatoes
1 small egg, beaten
1 tsp caster sugar
basil leaves, to garnish
crusty bread, to serve

Preheat the oven to 180°C/350°F/Gas Mark 4. Place the rice in a saucepan, pour over the vegetable stock and bring to the boil. Simmer for 30 minutes or until the rice is tender. Drain and turn into a mixing bowl.

Add 1 teaspoon of sunflower oil to a small nonstick pan and gently fry the shallot, garlic, pepper, chilli and mushrooms for 2 minutes. Add to the rice with the chopped oregano. Season with plenty of salt and pepper.

Slice the top off each tomato and reserve. Scoop out the flesh, removing the hard core. Pass the flesh through a sieve. Add 1 tablespoon of the juice to the rice mixture. Stir in the beaten egg and mix. Sprinkle a little sugar in the base of each tomato. Pile the rice mixture into the shells. Place the tomatoes in a baking dish and pour a little cold water around them. Replace their lids and drizzle a few drops of sunflower oil over the tops. Bake for about 25 minutes. Garnish with the basil leaves, season with black pepper and serve immediately with crusty bread.

If liked, keep one tomato for the next day: place on a plate, cover with clingfilm and refrigerate. It would be better to prepare the tomato but not to bake it until needed. Reheat cooked tomatoes in the microwave. Recover with clean clingfilm and pierce 2–3 times. Heat on High for 2 minutes, allow to stand for 1 minute. Check it is piping hot; if not, heat for a further minute.

Bulgur Wheat Salad with Minty Lemon Dressing

Makes 1 large portion

50 g/2 oz bulgur wheat
5 cm/2 inch piece cucumber
2 shallots, peeled
50 g/2 oz baby sweetcorn
3 ripe but firm cherry tomatoes

For the dressing:

1 tbsp grated lemon zest
2 tbsp lemon juice
1 tbsp freshly chopped mint
2 tsp freshly chopped parsley
1–2 tsp clear honey
2 tbsp vegetable or sunflower oil
salt and freshly ground
black pepper

Place the bulgur wheat in a saucepan and cover with boiling water.

Simmer for about 10 minutes, then drain thoroughly and turn into a serving bowl.

Cut the cucumber into small dice, chop the shallots finely and reserve. Steam the sweetcorn over a pan of boiling water for 10 minutes or until tender. Drain and slice into thick chunks.

Cut a cross on the top of each tomato and place in boiling water until their skins start to peel away. Remove the skins and the seeds and cut the tomatoes into small dice.

Make the dressing by briskly whisking all the ingredients in a small bowl until mixed well.

When the bulgur wheat has cooled a little, add all the prepared vegetables and stir in the dressing. Season to taste with salt and pepper and serve.

Any remaining salad can be kept in the refrigerator. Spoon into a clean bowl, cover with clingfilm and keep for up to 2 days. Stir before eating. Not suitable for freezing.

Roasted Mixed Vegetables with Garlic & Herb Sauce

Makes 2 portions

3–4 large garlic cloves
1 medium onion, peeled and cut into wedges
2 carrots, peeled and quartered
1 parsnip, peeled
3 small potatoes, scrubbed and halved
2 fresh rosemary sprigs
2 fresh thyme sprigs
2 tbsp olive or vegetable oil
salt and freshly ground black pepper
75 g/3 oz low-fat soft cheese with herbs and garlic
2 tbsp milk
zest of 1/2 lemon
thyme sprigs, to garnish

Preheat the oven to 220°C/425°F/Gas Mark 7. Cut the garlic cloves in half horizontally. Put into a large roasting tin with all the vegetables and herbs. Add the oil, season well with salt and pepper and toss together to coat lightly in the oil. Cover with kitchen foil and roast in the preheated oven for 30 minutes. Remove the kitchen foil and cook for a further 15 minutes or until all the vegetables are tender and slightly charred. Remove the tin from the oven and allow to cool.

In a small saucepan, melt the low-fat soft cheese together with the milk and lemon zest.

Remove the garlic from the roasting tin and squeeze the flesh into a bowl. Mash thoroughly then add to the sauce. Heat through gently. Season the vegetables to taste. Pour some sauce into a small ramekin and garnish with thyme sprigs. Serve immediately with the roasted vegetables and the sauce to dip.

This will not freeze well but will keep overnight in the refrigerator. Reheat gently either in the microwave on High for 1–2 minutes or in a saucepan on the hob, stirring frequently. Pour the sauce over to reheat.

Easy-peasy

Pasta

Noodles

Pasta and noodles are great; they're cheap to buy, last for ages in the cupboard, are quick to cook and go with pretty much anything. In this delicious selection we have both classics and more adventurous dishes, from pasta bakes and spaghetti to chow mein and spicy fried noodles, there is something to satisfy every craving. Some of these dishes also make enough for more than one meal – prefect for when you want an easy dinner to reheat.

Baked Macaroni Cheese

Makes 4 portions

350 g/12 oz macaroni
50 g/2 oz butter or margarine
1 onion, peeled and finely chopped
40 g/1 1/2 oz plain flour
600 ml/1 pt milk
1–2 dried or fresh bay leaves
salt and freshly ground black pepper
freshly grated nutmeg (optional)
1 tbsp Dijon or English mustard
125 g/4 oz mature
Cheddar cheese, grated
1 tbsp dried breadcrumbs (optional)
1 tbsp freshly grated Parmesan
cheese (optional)
basil sprig, to garnish (optional)

Preheat the oven to 190°C/375°F/Gas Mark 5, 10 minutes before cooking. Bring a large pan of lightly salted water to a rolling boil. Add the macaroni and cook according to the packet instructions, or until *al dente*. Drain thoroughly and reserve.

Meanwhile, melt the butter or margarine in a large, heavy-based saucepan, add the onion and cook, stirring frequently, for 5–7 minutes, until softened. Sprinkle in the flour and cook, stirring constantly, for 2 minutes. Remove from the heat, stir in the milk, return to the heat and cook, stirring, until a smooth sauce has formed. Add the bay leaf(ves) and season to taste with salt and pepper and nutmeg, if using. Simmer for about 5 minutes, stirring frequently. Remove from the heat, add the mustard and Cheddar cheese and stir until the cheese has melted. Stir in the macaroni then tip into a lightly oiled ovenproof dish. If using the breadcrumbs and Parmesan cheese, sprinkle over the macaroni. Bake in the preheated oven for 30–35 minutes until golden. Garnish with a basil sprig, if using, and serve immediately, removing the bay leaf(ves).

Spoon any uneaten portions into small dishes. Store in the refrigerator covered with clingfilm and use within 3 days. Reheat in a saucepan, adding a little more milk to thin down the sauce. Alternatively, wrap, label, date and freeze the dishes. Use within 1 month. Once thawed, reheat as above and adjust the seasoning as it may be altered by freezing.

Penne with Mixed Peppers & Garlic

Makes 1 large portion

1/2 each of green, red and
yellow peppers
2 tbsp olive or sunflower oil
1 small onion, peeled and sliced
1 garlic clove, peeled and crushed
2 rashers smoked streaky bacon,
finely chopped
150 ml/1/4 pint chicken stock
salt and freshly ground black pepper
125 g/4 oz fresh or dried penne
1 tsp freshly chopped parsley
2 tsp Parmesan or Cheddar cheese,
finely grated

To serve:
green salad
warm granary bread

Preheat the grill and line the grill rack with kitchen foil. Deseed the peppers and place cut side down on the grill rack. Cook under the grill until the skins become blistered and black all over. Place the peppers in a polythene bag and allow to cool, then discard the skin and slice thinly.

Heat the oil in a heavy-based pan. Add the onion, garlic and bacon and cook for 4–5 minutes, or until the onion has softened. Add the peppers and cook for 1 minute. Pour in the stock and season to taste with salt and pepper. Cover and simmer for 10 minutes.

Meanwhile, bring a large pan of lightly salted water to a rolling boil. Add the penne and cook according to the packet instructions, about 3–4 minutes, or until *al dente*. Drain thoroughly and return to the pan.

Pour the pepper sauce over the pasta and toss lightly. Tip into a warmed serving dish and sprinkle with the chopped parsley and grated cheese. Serve immediately with a green salad and warm granary bread.

Keep any remaining pasta and sauce in a clean bowl, covered with clingfilm overnight in the refrigerator. The next day reheat on High for 2 minutes in the microwave.

Gnocchetti with Broccoli & Bacon Sauce

Makes 1 large portion

125 g/4 oz broccoli florets
2 tbsp olive or sunflower oil
2 bacon rashers, finely chopped
1 small onion, peeled and
finely chopped
1–2 garlic cloves, peeled and sliced
150 ml/¼ pint milk
125 g/4 oz gnocchetti (little elongated
ribbed shells) or farfalle
25 g/1 oz freshly grated Parmesan or
Cheddar cheese, plus extra to serve
salt and freshly ground
black pepper

Bring a large pan of salted water to the boil. Add the broccoli florets and cook for about 8–10 minutes, or until very soft. Drain thoroughly, allow to cool slightly then chop finely and reserve.

Heat the olive or sunflower oil in a heavy-based pan, add the bacon and cook over a medium heat for 5 minutes, or until golden and crisp. Add the onion and cook for a further 5 minutes, or until soft and lightly golden. Add the garlic and cook for 1 minute.

Transfer the chopped broccoli to the bacon mixture and pour in the milk. Bring slowly to the boil and simmer rapidly for about 8–10 minutes, or until reduced to a creamy texture.

Meanwhile, bring a large pan of lightly salted water to the boil. Add the pasta and cook according to the packet instructions, or until *al dente*. Drain thoroughly, reserving a little of the cooking water. Add the pasta and cheese to the broccoli mixture. Stir, adding the reserved cooking water to make a creamy sauce. Season to taste and serve with extra cheese.

If liked, this recipe can be doubled up for a further meal. Make as above simply doubling the ingredients. Spoon into bowls, cover with clingfilm and store in the refrigerator for 2–3 days. When ready to eat, tip into a pan, add a little extra milk. Heat gently, stirring frequently until piping hot.

Vegetarian Spaghetti Bolognese

Serves 4

2 tbsp vegetable or olive oil
1 onion small, peeled and
finely chopped
1 small carrot, peeled and
finely chopped
1 small celery stalk, trimmed and
finely chopped
175 g/6 oz Quorn mince
200 ml/7 fl oz pint vegetable stock
1–2 tbsp tomato purée
75 g/3 oz dried spaghetti
4 tbsp natural Greek yoghurt
salt and freshly ground
black pepper
1 tbsp freshly chopped parsley

Heat the oil in a large saucepan and add the onion, carrot and celery. Cook gently for 5 minutes, until softened and starting to brown. Add the Quorn mince and cook for a further 2–3 minutes.

Add half the stock to the Quorn mixture along with the tomato purée. Cover and simmer gently for about 15 minutes, adding the remaining stock as necessary.

Meanwhile, bring a large pan of salted water to the boil and add the spaghetti. Cook until *al dente*, or according to the packet instructions. Drain well. Remove the sauce from the heat, add the yoghurt and season to taste with salt and pepper. Stir in the parsley and serve immediately with the pasta.

The sauce will keep well in the refrigerator for up to 3 days. Spoon into a dish and cover with clingfilm. I would not recommend keeping the spaghetti; cook this fresh as required. You could freeze the sauce for up to 1 month. Thaw before using.

To reheat, place the Bolognese sauce in a saucepan over a gentle heat. Add a little extra stock. Bring slowly to the boil and simmer for 5–8 minutes, stirring occasionally, until piping hot.

Chicken 🐝 Mushroom Lasagne

Makes 4 portions

1 tbsp olive or sunflower oil
225 g/8 oz button mushrooms,
wiped and sliced
15 g/^{1}/$_2$ oz butter or margarine
25 g/1 oz plain flour
300 ml/^{1}/$_2$ pint skimmed milk
1 bay leaf
225 g/8 oz cooked chicken, cubed
^{1}/$_4$ tsp freshly grated nutmeg
(optional)
salt and freshly ground black pepper
400 g can tomatoes, drained
and chopped
1 tsp dried mixed herbs
9 lasagne sheets (about 150 g/5 oz)

For the topping:

200 ml/7 fl oz 0%-fat Greek yogurt
1 medium egg, lightly beaten
1 tbsp finely grated
Parmesan cheese
mixed salad leaves, to serve

Preheat the oven to 180°C/350°F/Gas 4. Heat the oil and cook the mushrooms until tender and all the juices have evaporated. Remove and reserve. Put the butter or margarine, flour, milk and bay leaf in the pan. Slowly bring to the boil, stirring until thickened. Simmer for 2–3 minutes. Remove the bay leaf and stir in the mushrooms, chicken, nutmeg, salt and pepper.

Mix together the tomatoes, mixed herbs and season with salt and pepper. Spoon half into the base of a 1.7 litre/3 pint ovenproof dish or use four individual dishes. Top with 3 sheets of lasagne, breaking them to fit where necessary. Cover with half the chicken mixture. Repeat the layers, then arrange the remaining 3 sheets of pasta on top. Mix together the yogurt and egg. Spoon over the lasagne, spreading the mixture into the corners. Sprinkle with the Parmesan and bake in the preheated oven for 45 minutes. Serve with the mixed salad.

Any uneaten lasagne can be covered in clingfilm and stored overnight in the refrigerator. If freezing, do so preferably before it is baked: wrap in kitchen foil, label and date. Thaw overnight in the refrigerator and cook as per the recipe. Or, if you prefer to freeze after baking, spoon into small containers and cover, label and date. Keep for up to 1 month. Thaw in the refrigerator overnight. Reheat cooked lasagne in the microwave on a plate covered with clingfilm and pierced 2–3 times, on High for 2 minutes or until piping hot. Allow to stand for 1 minute before eating.

Fusilli Pasta with Spicy Tomato Salsa

Makes 1 large portion

2 medium ripe tomatoes
1 tbsp lemon juice
1 tbsp grated zest of 1 lemon
1 shallot, peeled and finely chopped
1–2 garlic cloves, peeled and
finely chopped
$1/2$–1 red chilli, depending on
heat tolerance
$1/2$–1 green chilli or $1/2$–1 tsp dried
crushed chillies
125 g/4 oz fresh or dried fusilli pasta
2 tbsp natural or Greek yogurt
2 tsp freshly chopped basil
(optional)
oregano sprig, to garnish (optional)

Place the tomatoes in a bowl and cover with boiling water. Allow to stand until the skins start to peel away. Remove the skins from the tomatoes, divide each tomato in four and remove all the seeds. Chop the flesh into small dice and put in a small pan. Add the lemon juice and zest and stir well. Add the chopped shallot and garlic.

If using the chillies remove the seeds carefully, chop the flesh finely and add to the pan. Or stir in the crushed chillies. Bring to the boil and simmer gently for 5–10 minutes until the salsa has thickened slightly. Reserve the salsa to allow the flavours to develop while the pasta is cooking.

Bring a large pan of water to the boil and add the pasta. Simmer gently for 3–4 minutes or until the pasta is just tender. Drain the pasta and rinse in boiling water. Top with a large spoonful of salsa and a small spoonful of yogurt. Garnish, if liked, with the chopped basil and oregano and serve immediately.

This dish is better if eaten immediately. The salsa would keep well in the refrigerator spooned into a small bowl, covered with clingfilm and used in 2–3 days.

Spaghetti with Turkey ✿ Bacon Sauce

Makes 1 large portion

125 g/4 oz spaghetti
1 tbsp butter or margarine
50 g/2 oz smoked streaky bacon,
rind removed
75 g/3 oz fresh turkey strips, if
preferred use chicken
1 small onion, peeled and chopped
1 garlic clove, peeled and chopped
1 medium egg, beaten
4 tbsp milk
salt and freshly ground
black pepper
1 tbsp freshly grated Parmesan or
Cheddar cheese
2 tsp freshly chopped coriander,
to garnish

Bring a large pan of lightly salted water to a rolling boil. Add the spaghetti and cook according to the packet instructions, or until *al dente*.

Meanwhile, melt the butter or margarine in a frying pan. Using a sharp knife cut the streaky bacon into small dice. Add the bacon to the pan with the turkey strips and cook for 8 minutes, or until browned, stirring occasionally to prevent sticking. Add the onion and garlic and cook for 5 minutes, or until softened, stirring occasionally.

Place the egg and milk in a bowl and season to taste with salt and pepper. Beat together then pour into the frying pan and cook, stirring, for 2 minutes or until the mixture begins to thicken but does not scramble.

Drain the spaghetti thoroughly and return to the pan. Pour over the sauce, add the grated cheese and toss lightly. Heat through for 2 minutes, or until piping hot. Tip into a warmed serving dish and sprinkle with freshly chopped coriander. Serve immediately.

If liked, the sauce can be made ahead so that when a quick meal is required all that has to be done is to cook the pasta and reheat the sauce. Use the sauce within 2 days; it is not suitable for freezing.

Spaghetti Bolognese

Makes 1 large portion

1 tbsp olive or sunflower oil
2 rashers unsmoked streaky bacon, rind removed and chopped
1 small onion, peeled and finely chopped
1 small carrot, peeled and finely chopped
½ celery stalk, trimmed and finely chopped
1 garlic clove, peeled and crushed
1 bay leaf (optional)
125 g/4 oz beef mince
200 g can tomatoes, chopped
1–2 tsp tomato purée
150 ml/¹/₄ pint beef stock
salt and freshly ground black pepper
125 g/ 4 oz spaghetti
freshly grated Parmesan or Cheddar cheese, to serve

Heat the olive or sunflower oil in a heavy-based pan, add the bacon and cook for 5 minutes or until slightly coloured. Add the onion, carrot, celery, garlic and bay leaf, if using, and cook, stirring, for 8 minutes, or until the vegetables are soft.

Add the beef mince to the pan and cook, stirring with a wooden spoon to break up any lumps in the meat, for 5–8 minutes, or until browned.

Stir the tomatoes and tomato purée into the mince and pour in the stock. Bring to the boil, lower the heat and simmer for 20 minutes, stirring occasionally. The longer you leave the sauce to cook, the more intense the flavour. Season to taste with salt and pepper and remove the bay leaf, if used.

Meanwhile, bring a large pan of lightly salted water to a rolling boil, add the spaghetti and cook for about 8 minutes or until *al dente*. Drain and arrange on warmed serving plates. Top with the prepared Bolognese sauce and serve immediately sprinkled with grated cheese.

The Bolognese sauce will keep well in the refrigerator covered with clingfilm for up to 3 days or will freeze, in a lidded container, for 1 month. Reheat in a saucepan until piping hot, or cover with clingfilm, pierce 2–3 times and heat on High in the microwave for 2 minutes or until piping hot.

Lasagne

Makes 4 portions

4 quantities prepared Bolognese
sauce (*see* page 128)
75 g/3 oz butter or margarine
4 tbsp plain flour
750 ml/1¼ pints milk
1 tsp readymade mustard
salt and freshly ground
black pepper
9 sheets lasagne
50g/2 oz freshly grated Parmesan
or Cheddar cheese
freshly chopped parsley, to garnish
(optional)
garlic bread, to serve

Preheat the oven to 200°C/400°F/Gas Mark 6, 15 minutes before cooking. Stir the prepared Bolognese sauce and reserve.

Melt the butter or margarine in a small heavy-based pan, add the flour and cook gently, stirring, for 2 minutes. Remove from the heat, gradually stir in the milk. Return to the heat and cook, stirring, for 2 minutes, or until the sauce thickens. Bring to the boil, remove from the heat and stir in the mustard. Season to taste. Butter a rectangular ovenproof dish and spread a thin layer of the white sauce over the base. Cover completely with three sheets of lasagne. Spoon a third of the prepared Bolognese sauce over the lasagne. Spoon over a third of the remaining white sauce, then sprinkle with a third of the grated cheese. Repeat the layers, finishing with cheese. Bake in the preheated oven for 30 minutes, or until golden-brown. Garnish, if liked, and serve immediately with warm garlic bread.

Store any uneaten lasagne in the refrigerator for up to 2 days. Spoon onto a clean plate or dish trying not to disturb the layers. Cover with clingfilm. Reheat in the microwave, covered with fresh clingfilm and heat on high for 2 minutes. Allow to stand for at least 1 minute before eating. If you want to freeze, this recipe will freeze well, but I would recommend freezing whole, unbaked (perfect for when parents are coming to visit). Make the recipe as above, but don't bake, then freeze for up to 1 month. It would be better to open freeze then wrap, label and date. When ready to eat, thaw overnight in the refrigerator and bake as above.

Sausage ❧ Redcurrant Pasta Bake

Makes 1 portion

2 good quality, thick pork sausages
1 tsp sunflower or olive oil
1 small onion, peeled and sliced
2 tsp plain white flour
300 ml/$^1/_2$ pint chicken stock
1 tsp freshly chopped thyme leaves,
plus sprigs to garnish
1 bay leaf (optional)
4 tsp redcurrant jelly
salt and freshly ground
black pepper
125 g/4 oz fresh penne
1 tbsp grated cheese

Prick the sausages, place under a preheated grill and cook for 15 minutes, turning frequently. Alternatively, cook them on the hob in a nonstick frying pan for 15 minutes, turning frequently or until golden brown. (There is no need to add any oil or fat, the fat in the sausages will be enough.) Reserve and wipe the frying pan clean if necessary.

Heat the oil in the frying pan, add the sliced onion and fry for 5 minutes, or until golden-brown. Stir in the flour and cook for 2 minutes. Remove the pan from the heat and gradually stir in the chicken stock. Return the pan to the heat and bring to the boil, stirring continuously until the sauce starts to thicken. Add the thyme, bay leaf, if using, and redcurrant jelly and season well with salt and pepper. Simmer the sauce for 3 minutes.

Bring a large pan of salted water to a rolling boil, add the pasta and cook for about 4 minutes, or until *al dente*. Drain thoroughly and reserve. Heat the oven to 200°C/400°F/Gas Mark 6 and place the sausages in an ovenproof dish. Add the pasta then pour over the sauce, removing the bay leaf, if used, and toss together. Sprinkle with the cheese and cook in the oven for 15–20 minutes, or until bubbling and golden-brown. Serve immediately, garnished with thyme sprigs.

The sauce and sausages will keep well overnight in the refrigerator, covered. To finish the dish, add cooked pasta and cheese, cover wih foil and cook as above, removing the foil for the last 10 minutes.

Warm Noodle Salad

Makes 2 portions

40 g/1¹/₂ oz smooth peanut butter
1¹/₂ tbsp sesame or sunflower oil
2 tsp light soy sauce
1 tbsp vinegar
1 tsp freshly grated root ginger
125 g/4 oz Chinese fine egg noodles
25 g/1 oz beansprouts
50 g/2 oz baby sweetcorn
50 g/2 oz carrots, peeled and cut into matchsticks
50 g/2 oz mangetout
50 g/2 oz cucumber, cut into thin strips
2 spring onions, trimmed and finely shredded

Place the peanut butter, 1 tablespoon of the oil, the soy sauce, vinegar and ginger in a food processor or glass bowl. Blend until smooth, then stir in 2 tablespoons hot water and blend again until smooth, adding a little extra water if necessary. Pour the dressing into a jug and reserve.

Bring a saucepan of lightly salted water to the boil, add the noodles and beansprouts and cook for 4 minutes, or according to the packet instructions. Drain, rinse under cold running water and drain again. Stir in the remaining oil and keep warm.

Bring a saucepan of lightly salted water to the boil and add the baby sweetcorn, carrots and mangetout and cook for 3–4 minutes, or until just tender but still crisp. Drain and cut the mangetout in half. Slice the baby sweetcorn (if very large) into 2–3 pieces and arrange on a warmed serving dish with the noodles. Add the cucumber strips and spring onions. Spoon over a little of the dressing and serve immediately with the remaining dressing.

This dish is best eaten immediately but can be eaten cold. Keep covered with clingfilm in the refrigerator overnight and eat as a cold salad the next day. It would not freeze well.

Pork Fried Noodles

Makes 2 portions

75 g/3 oz dried thread egg noodles
50 g/2 oz broccoli florets
2 tbsp groundnut or vegetable oil
175 g/6 oz lean pork such as tenderloin,
cut into slices
2 tbsp soy sauce
1 tbsp lemon juice
pinch sugar
1 tsp chilli sauce
1 tbsp sesame oil (optional)
small piece fresh root ginger,
peeled and cut into sticks
1 garlic clove, peeled and chopped
½ green chilli, deseeded and sliced
50 g/2 oz mangetout, halved
2 small eggs, lightly beaten
125 g/4 oz can water chestnuts,
drained and sliced (optional)

To garnish:

radish rose
spring onion tassels

Place the noodles in a bowl and cover with boiling water. Leave to stand for 20 minutes, stirring occasionally, or until tender. Drain and reserve. Meanwhile, blanch the broccoli in a saucepan of lightly salted boiling water for 2 minutes. Drain, refresh under cold running water and reserve.

Heat a large wok or frying pan, add the groundnut oil and heat until just smoking. Add the pork and stir-fry for 5 minutes, or until browned. Using a slotted spoon, remove the pork slices and reserve. Mix together the soy sauce, lemon juice, sugar, chilli sauce and sesame oil and reserve.

Add the ginger to the wok or frying pan and stir-fry for 30 seconds. Add the garlic and chilli and stir-fry for 30 seconds. Add the reserved broccoli and stir-fry for 3 minutes. Stir in the mangetout, pork and reserved noodles with the beaten eggs and water chestnuts, if using, and stir-fry for 5 minutes or until heated through. Pour over the reserved chilli sauce, toss well and turn into a warmed serving dish. Garnish and serve immediately.

This dish will be fine to eat cold the next day. Spoon into a clean dish or bowl, cover with clingfilm and store overnight in the refrigerator.

Chicken with Noodles

Makes 2 large portions

125 g/4 oz medium egg noodles
125 g/4 oz skinless, boneless
chicken breast fillets
1 tbsp light soy sauce
2 tsp vinegar
5 tsp groundnut or vegetable oil
2 garlic cloves, peeled and
finely chopped
50 g/2 oz mangetout
25 g/1 oz smoked back bacon, cut
into fine strips
$\frac{1}{2}$ tsp sugar
2 spring onions, peeled
and finely chopped
1 tsp sesame oil (optional)

Cook the noodles according to the packet instructions. Drain and refresh under cold water. Drain again and reserve.

Slice the chicken into fine shreds and mix with 2 teaspoons of the light soy sauce and vinegar. Leave to marinate in the refrigerator for 10 minutes.

Heat a wok or large frying pan, add 2 teaspoons of the oil and, when hot, stir-fry the chicken shreds for about 2 minutes, then transfer to a plate. Wipe the wok clean with absorbent kitchen paper.

Return the wok or frying pan to the heat and add the remaining oil. Add the garlic, then after 10 seconds add the mangetout and bacon. Stir-fry for a further 1 minute, then add the drained noodles, remaining soy sauce, sugar and spring onions. Stir-fry for a further 2 minutes, then add the reserved chicken.

Stir-fry for a further 3–4 minutes until the chicken is cooked through. Add the sesame oil, if using, and mix together. Serve either hot or cold.

This dish would keep overnight in the refrigerator, but do not freeze. Place in a bowl or dish and cover with clingfilm. Use the next day, cold.

Turkey Chow Mein

Makes 2 portions

125 g/4 oz fine egg noodles
2 tbsp groundnut or vegetable oil
2 tsp light soy sauce
1 tbsp Chinese rice wine
or malt vinegar
125 g/4 oz turkey steak, cut
into strips
1–2 garlic cloves, peeled and
finely chopped
50 g/2 oz mangetout, finely sliced
50 g/2 oz cooked ham, cut into
fine strips
2 tsp dark soy sauce
pinch sugar

To garnish (optional):
shredded spring onions
toasted sesame seeds

Place the egg noodles in a large bowl and cover with boiling water. Leave for 3–5 minutes, drain and add 1 teaspoon of the oil and stir lightly. Reserve. Place the light soy sauce, 1 tablespoon of the Chinese rice wine or vinegar and 1 teaspoon of the oil in a bowl. Add the turkey and stir well. Cover lightly and leave to marinate in the refrigerator for about 15 minutes. Heat the wok or large frying pan over a high heat, add 2 teaspoons of oil and, when very hot, add the turkey and its marinade and stir-fry for 2 minutes. Remove the turkey and juices and reserve. Wipe the wok or frying pan clean with absorbent kitchen paper.

Reheat the wok or frying pan and add 1 tablespoon of the oil. Add the garlic and toss in the oil for 20 seconds. Add the mangetout and the ham and stir-fry for 1 minute. Add the noodles, Chinese rice wine or vinegar, dark soy sauce and sugar. Season to taste with salt and pepper and stir-fry for 2 minutes. Add the turkey and juices and stir-fry for 4 minutes, or until the turkey is cooked. Garnish with spring onions and sesame seeds, if using, and serve.

This dish will not freeze well. Refrigerate in a clean dish and covered with clingfilm. Use the next day, hot or cold. To reheat, heat 1–2 teaspoons oil in a frying pan. When hot, add the chow mein and cook over a medium heat for 10–12 minutes until the turkey is piping hot. Stir frequently. Or, cover with clean clingfilm, pierce the top and heat on High for 2 minutes in the microwave. Allow to stand for 1 minute. Ensure that the turkey is piping hot.

Curries 🙦 Rice Dishes

🙦

This chapter will show you how to make all manner of delicious curries yourself quickly and easily – so there's no need for loads of greasy and expensive takeaways. Here we provide a diverse selection ranging from variations on classic baltis and kormas to Thai and Caribbean-style dishes. Or, if curries aren't your thing, there's a great selection of rice-based dishes, Sausage & Bacon Risotto and Aduki Bean & Rice Burgers are just a few to try.

Chicken & Lentil Curry

Makes 1 large portion

2–3 chicken thighs, depending on appetite, skinned
2 tsp sunflower or vegetable oil
40 g/1^1/$_2$ oz split red lentils
2–3 tsp mild curry paste
1 bay leaf (optional)
small strip of lemon zest
300 ml/^{1}/$_2$ pint chicken or vegetable stock
40 g/1^1/$_2$ oz spinach leaves, rinsed; shredded, if liked
1 tsp freshly chopped coriander (optional)
2 tsp lemon juice
salt and freshly ground black pepper

To serve:

freshly cooked rice
low-fat natural yogurt

Secure the chicken thighs with cocktail sticks to keep their shape. Heat the oil in a nonstick frying pan, add the chicken and fry for 5 minutes, turning frequently until browned all over, remove from the pan and reserve.

Put the lentils in a sieve and rinse thoroughly under cold running water. Place in a saucepan then stir in the curry paste, bay leaf, if using, lemon zest and stock. Stir, and then slowly bring to the boil. Turn down the heat to a gentle simmer, half-cover the pan with a lid and cook for 5 minutes, stirring occasionally. Place the chicken in the pan with the lentils and half-cover. Simmer for 20 minutes. Stir in the spinach and cook for a further 5 minutes or until the chicken is very tender and the sauce is thick. Remove the bay leaf, if using, and lemon zest. Stir in the coriander and lemon juice, then season to taste with salt and pepper. Serve immediately with the rice and a little natural yogurt.

Any leftover curry can be kept, covered with clingfilm, in the refrigerator overnight. Ensure that the chicken is thoroughly reheated before eating. Reheat if possible in the microwave. Cover with fresh clingfilm, pierce the film 2–3 times and heat on High for 3 minutes 20 seconds. Allow to stand for 2 minutes before eating. If not using a microwave, place the curry in a saucepan and bring to the boil. Reduce to a simmer, cover with a lid and cook for 10–12 minutes, stirring frequently to prevent it burning before eating; ensure that it is piping hot.

Spinach Dhal

Makes 1 large portion

40 g/1^1/$_2$ oz split red lentils
1 small onion, peeled
and chopped
50 g/2 oz potato, peeled and cut
into small chunks
^{1}/$_2$ green chilli, deseeded
and chopped
150 ml/^{1}/$_4$ pint water
^{1}/$_2$ tsp turmeric
125 g/4 oz fresh spinach
1 medium tomato, chopped
2 tsp vegetable oil
1 tsp mustard seeds (optional)

Rinse the lentils and place in a saucepan with the onion, potato, chilli, water and turmeric. Bring to the boil, then reduce the heat, cover and simmer for 15 minutes, or until the lentils are tender and most of the liquid has been absorbed.

Chop the spinach and add to the pan with the tomato and cook for a further 5 minutes, or until the spinach has wilted.

Heat the oil in a frying pan, add the mustard seeds, and fry for 1 minute, or until they pop. Stir into the dhal and serve.

The dhal will keep well if placed in a clean bowl, covered with clingfilm and left in the refrigerator. Use within 3 days.

To freeze, place the cooked dhal in a container or freezer bag and place in the freezer, not forgetting to label and date. Keep for up to 1 month. When ready to eat, thaw completely overnight in the refrigerator then heat on High for 2 minutes, stirring halfway through the reheating time. Alternatively, reheat in a saucepan over a low heat, stirring frequently, for 5–8 minutes. Ensure the dhal is piping hot before eating.

Thai Green Chicken Curry

Makes 2 portions

1 small onion, peeled and chopped
1 lemon grass stalk, outer leaves
discarded and finely sliced
(optional)
1 garlic clove, peeled and
finely chopped
1 tbsp freshly grated root ginger
1 green chilli
zest and juice of $\frac{1}{2}$ lemon
2 tbsp groundnut or vegetable oil
1–2 tsp Thai fish sauce (optional)
1 tbsp freshly chopped coriander
1 tbsp freshly chopped basil
175 g/6 oz skinless, boneless chicken
breasts cut into strips
50 g /2 oz fine green beans, trimmed
200 ml can coconut milk
fresh basil leaves, to garnish
(optional)
freshly cooked rice, to serve

Place the onion, lemon grass, if using, garlic, ginger, chilli, lemon zest and juice, 1 tablespoon of the oil, the fish sauce, if using, coriander and basil in a bowl. Using a handheld blender (or food processor), blend to a form a smooth paste, which should be of a spoonable consistency. If the sauce looks thick, add a little water. Remove and reserve.

Heat the wok or large frying pan, add the remaining 1 tablespoon of oil and, when hot, add the chicken. Stir-fry for 2–3 minutes, until the chicken starts to colour, then add the green beans and stir-fry for a further minute. Remove the chicken and beans from the wok or frying pan and reserve. Wipe the wok or frying pan clean with absorbent kitchen paper.

Spoon the reserved green paste into the wok or frying pan and heat for 1 minute. Add the coconut milk and whisk to blend. Return the chicken and beans to the wok or frying pan and bring to the boil. Simmer for 5–7 minutes, or until the chicken is cooked. Sprinkle with basil leaves, if using, and serve immediately with freshly cooked rice.

This curry would be super to share with a friend, but it can be kept overnight in the refrigerator in a clean bowl. Cover with clingfilm and use within 2 days. I would not recommend freezing, as the delicate flavour could be lost.

Kerala Pork Curry

Makes 1 large portion

125 g/4 oz lean pork such as fillet
or loin, trimmed
1 tbsp vegetable oil
2 tsp desiccated coconut
1 tsp mustard seeds
1 cinnamon stick, bruised
$^1/_2$ tsp ground cumin
$^1/_2$ tsp ground coriander
1 red chilli, deseeded and chopped
1–2 garlic cloves, peeled
and chopped
1 small onion, peeled and chopped
$^1/_2$ tsp saffron strands or turmeric
150 ml/$^1/_4$ pint coconut milk, or use
a small piece of creamed coconut
blended with warm water
50 ml/2 fl oz water
50 g/2 oz frozen peas
freshly cooked basmati rice, to serve

Cut the pork into small chunks and reserve. Heat 1 teaspoon of the oil in a frying pan; add the desiccated coconut and fry for 30 seconds, stirring, until lightly toasted. Reserve.

Add the remaining oil to the pan, add the seeds and fry for 30 seconds, or until they pop. Add the remaining spices and cook, stirring, for 2 minutes. Add the pork and fry for 5 minutes, or until sealed. Add the chilli, garlic and onion and continue to fry for 3 minutes before stirring in the saffron or turmeric blended with a teaspoon of water. Stir, then pour in the coconut milk and water. Bring to the boil then reduce the heat, cover and simmer, stirring occasionally, for 30 minutes. Add a little more water if the liquid is evaporating quickly. Turn the heat down slightly, then add the peas and cook for a further 10 minutes before serving with freshly cooked basmati rice.

If you have some of this delicious curry left, spoon into a bowl, cover with clingfilm and keep for up to two days in the refrigerator. To reheat, re-cover the bowl with clean clingfilm and heat on High for 2 minutes 20 seconds in the microwave until piping hot, allowing to stand for 2 minutes before stirring and serving. Or, reheat in a saucepan: spoon into the pan, place over a gentle heat and bring to the boil; reduce the heat to a simmer, cover with a lid and cook for 10–12 minutes, stirring frequently, until piping hot. Add a little extra water if drying out. The curry will freeze, but the flavour will not be so intense. Keep in the freezer no longer than 1 month.

Curried Potatoes with Spinach

Makes 1 large portion

150 g/5 oz potatoes, peeled
1/2 tsp cumin seeds or ground cumin
2 tsp vegetable oil
1 small onion, peeled and chopped
1 garlic clove, peeled and crushed
1/2–1 red chilli, depending on
heat tolerance, deseeded and
finely chopped
1/2 tsp ground coriander
1/2 tsp turmeric
2 medium tomatoes
125 g/4 oz fresh leaf spinach, lightly
rinsed and chopped
25 ml/1 fl oz water
1–2 tsp salt and freshly ground
black pepper

Cut the potatoes into small cubes and reserve. Dry-fry the cumin seeds, if using, in a saucepan for 30 seconds, then add the oil, potatoes and ground cumin, if using. Cook for 3–5 minutes, stirring, or until the potatoes are beginning to turn golden.

Add the onion, garlic and chilli and continue to cook for 2–3 minutes, or until the onion is beginning to soften. Sprinkle in the ground coriander and turmeric and cook for a further 2 minutes.

Chop the tomatoes and stir into the pan. Cover and cook, stirring occasionally, for 10 minutes, or until the potatoes are tender. Stir in the spinach, water and seasoning, to taste, and cook for 2 minutes, or until the spinach has wilted, then serve.

Any leftover potatoes can be kept overnight in the refrigerator. Place in a clean dish and cover with clingfilm. They would not freeze well. They can then be reheated in the microwave covered with clean clingfilm, which has been pierced 2–3 times – heat on High for 1 minute or until piping hot. Or, they could be fried in a little oil, stirring frequently, for 5 minutes. They would also be good if eaten cold.

Malaysian Fish Curry

Makes 2 portions

2 firm fish fillets, such as fresh
haddock or coley, 125 g/4 oz each
in weight
1 tbsp groundnut or vegetable oil
2 garlic cloves, peeled and crushed
2.5 cm/1 inch piece fresh root
ginger, peeled and grated
1 tsp turmeric
1 tsp ground coriander
1 tbsp mild or medium Madras curry
paste, depending on taste
250 ml/8 fl oz coconut milk
1 tbsp freshly chopped coriander
lime or lemon wedges, to
garnish (optional)
stir-fried oriental vegetables and
fragrant rice, to serve

Preheat the oven to 180°C/350°F/Gas Mark 4. Lightly rinse the fish fillets and pat dry with absorbent kitchen paper. Place in a lightly oiled ovenproof dish.

Heat the oil in a frying pan, add the garlic and ginger and fry for 2 minutes. Add the turmeric, ground coriander and curry paste and cook for a further 3 minutes, stirring frequently. Take off the heat and gradually stir in the coconut milk. Cool slightly, then pour over the fish. Cover with lightly buttered kitchen foil and cook in the preheated oven for 20 minutes, or until the fish is tender. Sprinkle with chopped coriander, and then garnish with lime or lemon wedges, if using, and serve with stir-fried vegetables and freshly cooked rice.

If liked, one of the cooked fillets could be kept to eat the next day. Cook and allow to cool before covering with clingfilm and placing in the refrigerator overnight. Or, the cooked fish could be frozen, but the flavour will not be as intense. If wishing to freeze, wrap in kitchen foil, label, date and freeze for up to 1 month. To reheat, ensure the fish is thoroughly thawed if frozen. Place on a plate, cover with clingfilm and pierce 2–3 times. Heat on High for 1 minute 20 seconds, allow to stand for 1 minute, then eat.

Lamb Balti

Makes 2 portions

225 g/8 oz lean lamb, such as neck
fillet, trimmed
2 tsp vegetable oil
1 tsp mustard seeds (optional)
$1/2$ tsp ground coriander
$1/2$ tsp ground cumin
$1/2$ tsp turmeric
$1/2$ tsp garam masala
1–2 garlic cloves, peeled
and crushed
1–2 green chillies, depending on heat
tolerance, deseeded and chopped
1 onion, peeled and chopped
$1/2$–1 small aubergine, trimmed
and chopped
2 tomatoes, chopped
1 tsp tomato purée
450 ml/$3/4$ pint lamb or
vegetable stock
2 tsp freshly chopped coriander
naan bread, to serve

Dice the lamb and reserve. Heat the oil in a large frying pan, add the mustard seeds, if using, and fry for 30 seconds, or until they pop.

Add the remaining spices to the pan and cook for 2 minutes, stirring throughout, before adding the garlic, chillies, onion and aubergine. Cook, stirring, for a further 5 minutes, or until the vegetables are coated in the spices.

Add the lamb and continue to fry for 5–8 minutes, or until sealed. Stir in the chopped tomatoes. Blend the tomato purée with the stock then pour into the pan. Bring to the boil, cover, reduce the heat and simmer for 45–50 minutes, or until the lamb is tender. Sprinkle with chopped coriander and serve with plenty of naan bread.

Any remaining balti will keep well overnight in the refrigerator. Spoon into a clean bowl, cover with clingfilm and place in the refrigerator. It will also freeze well. Keep for up to 1 month. Reheat in the microwave on High for 2 minutes 30 seconds. Stand for 1 minute; if not piping hot, reheat for a further minute, stand for 1 minute then eat. Or, reheat in a saucepan on the hob for 10–12 minutes, stir well and ensure it is piping hot before eating. Balti is meant to be a wet curry so if there is not much liquid when reheating add a little water or stock.

Caribbean-style Chicken Stew

Makes 2 portions

4 skinless, boneless chicken portions,
each about 125 g/4 oz in weight
1 tbsp groundnut or vegetable oil
1 celery stalk, trimmed (optional)
3 baby onions, peeled and halved
1–2 garlic cloves, peeled and sliced
1/2 habanero chilli, deseeded and
sliced or 1/2–1 tsp dried
crushed chillies
1/2 tsp ground cumin
1/4 tsp ground coriander
1/2 tsp turmeric
2 tsp demerara sugar
2 medium tomatoes, chopped
450 ml/3/4 pint chicken stock
1 tsp freshly chopped coriander
sweet potato mash (optional)
to serve

Lightly rinse the chicken and dry with absorbent kitchen paper. Heat the oil in a large saucepan or frying pan add the chicken and brown on all sides. Remove and reserve.

Chop the celery and add to the pan with the onions, garlic and chilli. Fry for 5–8 minutes then add all the spices and cook for a further 3 minutes. Add the sugar, tomatoes and stock and bring to the boil.

Return the chicken to the pan, then reduce the heat, cover and simmer for 1 hour, or until the chicken is tender. Spoon into a warmed serving dish, sprinkle with chopped coriander and serve with the sweet potato mash, if using.

Any remaining chicken can be kept in the refrigerator overnight. Place on a clean plate and cover with clingfilm. Use within 2 days. It will also freeze for up to 1 month. Place in a freezer bag, label and date. Thaw in the refrigerator.

To reheat, place the chicken in a saucepan with a lid. Heat on the hob for 10–12 minutes until piping hot.

Thai-style Cauliflower & Potato Curry

Makes 1 portion

125 g/4 oz new potatoes, peeled
and halved or quartered
75 g/3 oz cauliflower florets
1 garlic clove, peeled and crushed
1 small onion, peeled and
finely chopped
15 g/^{1}/$_2$ oz ground almonds
^{1}/$_2$ tsp ground coriander
pinch ground cumin
^{1}/$_2$ tsp turmeric
1 tbsp vegetable oil
salt and freshly ground
black pepper
15 g/^{1}/$_2$ oz creamed coconut, broken
into small pieces
150 ml/^{1}/$_2$ pint vegetable stock
1–2 tsp mango chutney
sprigs of fresh coriander, to garnish
freshly cooked long-grain rice,
to serve

Bring a saucepan of lightly salted water to the boil, add the potatoes and cook for 15 minutes or until just tender. Drain and leave to cool. Boil the cauliflower for 2 minutes, then drain and refresh under cold running water. Drain again and reserve.

Meanwhile, blend the garlic, onion, ground almonds and spices with 2 tablespoons of the oil, and salt and pepper to taste in a food processor until a smooth paste is formed. Heat a wok or frying pan, add the remaining oil and, when hot, add the spice paste and cook for 3–4 minutes, stirring continuously.

Dissolve the creamed coconut in 3 tablespoons of boiling water and add to the wok or frying pan. Pour in the stock, cook for 2–3 minutes, then stir in the cooked potatoes and cauliflower.

Stir in the mango chutney and heat through for 3–4 minutes, or until piping hot. Tip into a warmed serving dish, garnish with sprigs of fresh coriander, if using, and serve immediately with freshly cooked rice.

This dish will not keep or reheat very well so only cook the amount you can eat, or invite a friend round to share.

Paneer ❀ Pea Curry

Makes 2 portions

75 g/3 oz paneer
150 ml/¼ pint vegetable oil, for deep frying, plus 1 tbsp oil
1 onion, peeled and chopped
1 garlic cloves, peeled and chopped
½–1 red chilli, deseeded and chopped or
¼–½ tsp dried crushed chilli
1–2 tsp medium curry powder
2 tomatoes, chopped
150 g/5 oz sugar snap peas or 75g /3 oz thawed frozen peas
50 ml/2 fl oz water (optional)
2 tbsp double cream or small piece creamed coconut dissolved in 2 tbsp warm water
2 tsp freshly chopped coriander (optional)

Cut the paneer into small cubes. Heat the oil in a deep fryer to a temperature of 180°C/350°F then deep-fry the paneer cubes for 3–4 minutes, or until golden brown. Drain on absorbent kitchen paper and reserve.

Heat 1 tablespoon of oil in a frying pan; add the onion, garlic and chilli and fry for 5 minutes, stirring frequently, until slightly softened. Sprinkle in the curry powder.

Stir in the chopped tomatoes and peas and continue to cook for 10 minutes, or until the peas are tender. Stir in a little water if the mixture is getting too dry. Add the fried paneer and heat for 2–3 minutes before stirring in the cream or coconut. Heat gently for 2–3 minutes, then stir in the chopped coriander, if using. Serve.

This dish will not keep or reheat very well so only cook the amount you can eat, or invite a friend round to share.

Egg ❧ Aubergine Curry

Makes 1 large portion

2 medium eggs
1 tbsp vegetable oil
1 onion, peeled and chopped
1 garlic clove, finely chopped
$1/2$–1 green chilli, deseeded and
finely chopped
small piece fresh root ginger,
peeled and grated
1 tsp medium hot curry powder
$1/2$ tsp turmeric
$1/2$ tsp ground coriander
125 g/4 oz baby aubergines trimmed
or 1 small aubergine
200 g/7 oz canned tomatoes,
chopped
2 tbsp double cream or small piece
creamed coconut blended with
2 tbsp water
1 tbsp freshly chopped coriander

Place the eggs in a saucepan and cover with cold water. Bring to the boil and continue to boil for 10 minutes. Drain and plunge into cold water and leave until cold. Drain, shell and reserve.

Heat the oil in a saucepan, add the onions, garlic, chilli and ginger and cook for 5 minutes, or until the onion has softened. Add the spices and continue to cook for a further 5 minutes.

Halve the baby aubergines, or chop the small aubergine into chunks, and add to the pan with the chopped tomatoes then simmer gently, stirring occasionally, for 12–15 minutes, or until the aubergine is tender. Stir in the cream or coconut milk and cook for a further 3 minutes. Cut the eggs into quarters, add to the pan and stir gently. Heat for 2 minutes before sprinkling with chopped coriander and serving.

This dish will not keep or reheat very well so only cook the amount you can eat.

Sweet & Sour Pork

Makes 1 large portion

1 small egg white
2 tsp cornflour
150 g/5 oz lean pork, such as fillet,
trimmed and cubed
300 ml/½ pint vegetable oil
1 small onion, peeled and finely
cut into sticks
1 medium carrot, peeled
and cut into matchsticks
small piece fresh root ginger, peeled
and cut into thin strips
85 ml/3 fl oz orange juice
85 ml/3 fl oz chicken stock
1 tsp light soy sauce
1 tbsp pineapple pieces (from 200 g
can), drained with juice reserved
1 tsp vinegar or 2 tsp lemon juice
1 tsp freshly chopped parsley
freshly cooked rice, to serve

In a bowl, whisk the egg white and cornflour, then add the pork to the mixture and stir until the cubes are well coated. Heat a wok or large frying pan, then add the oil and heat until very hot before adding the pork and stir-frying for 30 seconds. Turn off the heat and continue to stir for 3 minutes. The meat should be white and sealed. Drain off the oil into a bowl, reserve the pork and wipe the wok or frying pan clean.

Pour 2 teaspoons of the drained oil back into the wok or frying pan and cook the onion, carrot and ginger for 2–3 minutes. Blend the orange juice with the stock, soy sauce and make up to 200 ml/7 fl oz with the reserved pineapple juice. Return the pork to the pan with the pineapple juice mixture and simmer for 3–4 minutes. Stir in the pineapple pieces and vinegar or lemon juice. Heat through, then sprinkle with the chopped parsley and serve immediately with freshly cooked rice.

Any remaining pork and sauce can be spooned into a small bowl, covered with clingfilm and kept in the refrigerator; use within 2 days. It could also be frozen with any remaining rice for up to 1 month. If the pork was frozen, ensure that it is thoroughly thawed before reheating. Stir well, then place on a plate with any thawed rice. Cover with clingfilm and pierce the top 2–3 times. Heat on high for 2 minutes. Check the plate feels piping hot underneath. If not, heat for a further minute. Allow to stand for 1 minute, then stir and eat.

Rice Nuggets in Herby Tomato Sauce

Makes 2 portions

300 ml/½ pint vegetable stock
1 bay leaf
75 g/3 oz arborio rice
25 g/1 oz Cheddar cheese, grated
1 small egg yolk
1 tsp plain flour
2 tsp freshly chopped parsley
grated Parmesan or extra Cheddar cheese, to serve

For the herby tomato sauce:

1 tsp olive oil
1 small onion, peeled and thinly sliced
1 garlic clove, peeled and crushed
½ small yellow pepper, deseeded and diced
200 g can tomatoes, chopped
1 tsp freshly chopped basil

Pour the stock into a large saucepan. Add the bay leaf. Bring to the boil, add the rice, stir, then cover and simmer for 15 minutes. Uncover, reduce the heat to low and cook for a further 5 minutes until the rice is tender and all the stock is absorbed, stirring frequently towards the end of cooking time. Cool. Remove the bay leaf. Stir the cheese, egg yolk, flour and parsley into the rice. Season to taste, then shape into 10 walnut-sized balls. Cover and refrigerate.

To make the sauce, heat the oil in a large frying pan and cook the onion for 5 minutes. Add the garlic and yellow pepper and cook for a further 5 minutes, until soft. Stir in the chopped tomatoes and simmer gently for 3 minutes. Stir in the chopped basil. Add the rice nuggets to the sauce and simmer for a further 10 minutes, or until the nuggets are cooked through and the sauce has reduced a little. Spoon onto plates and serve hot, sprinkled with grated cheese.

Any leftover nuggets can be kept in the refrigerator. Place in a dish with the sauce, cover with clingfilm and use within 2 days. Reheat the nuggets in the microwave on High for 2 minutes, allow to stand for 1 minute and eat while still hot. Or, cover with kitchen foil and reheat in a moderate oven (180°C/350°F/Gas Mark 4) for 20–25 minutes. Stir the sauce occasionally and do not allow it to dry out – add a little stock or water if necessary.

Thai Coconut Chicken

Makes 2 portions

$^1/_2$ tsp cumin seeds
$^1/_2$ tsp mustard seeds
$^1/_2$ tsp coriander seeds
$^1/_2$ tsp turmeric
1 bird's-eye chilli, deseeded and
finely chopped
1 tbsp freshly grated root ginger
1 garlic clove, peeled and
finely chopped
50 ml/2 fl oz double cream
2 skinless chicken thighs
2 tbsp groundnut or vegetable oil
1 medium onion, peeled and
finely sliced
150 ml/$^1/_4$ pint coconut milk
salt and freshly ground
black pepper
2–4 tbsp chopped coriander
2 spring onions,
shredded, to garnish
freshly cooked Thai fragrant rice,
to serve

Heat the wok or large frying pan and add the cumin seeds, mustard seeds and coriander seeds. Dry-fry over a low to medium heat for 2 minutes, or until the fragrance becomes stronger and the seeds start to pop. Add the turmeric and leave to cool slightly. Grind the spices in a pestle and mortar, or a small grinder, to a fine powder.

Mix the chilli, ginger, garlic and the cream together in a small bowl, add the ground spices and mix. Place the chicken thighs in a shallow dish and spread the spice paste over the thighs. Heat the wok or large frying pan over a high heat, add the oil and, when hot, add the onion and stir-fry until golden brown. Add the chicken and the spice paste. Cook for 5–6 minutes, stirring occasionally, until evenly coloured. Add the coconut milk and season to taste with salt and pepper. Simmer the chicken for 15–20 minutes until the thighs are cooked through, taking care not to allow the mixture to boil. Stir in the chopped coriander and serve immediately with the freshly cooked rice, sprinkled with shredded spring onions.

It is worth making double and freezing half. When cooked, cool the chicken to be frozen then place in a container with the sauce. Label and date, then freeze for up to 1 month. Allow to thaw completely in the refrigerator. It will also keep for 2–3 days in the refrigerator. To reheat, place in a frying pan with a lid or a medium-sized saucepan. Cook over a gentle heat for 10–12 minutes until piping hot. Add a little extra coconut milk if there is not much sauce.

Rice-filled Peppers

Makes 2 portions

3 ripe tomatoes
1 tbsp vegetable or olive oil
1 small onion, peeled and chopped
1 garlic clove, peeled and crushed
$1/2$ tsp sugar
50 g/2 oz cooked long-grain rice
25 g/1 oz pine nuts or chopped
nuts, toasted
1 tsp freshly chopped oregano
salt and freshly ground black pepper
2 peppers

To serve:

mixed salad and warm, crusty bread

Preheat the oven to 200°C/400°F/Gas Mark 6. Put the tomatoes in a small bowl and pour over boiling water to cover. Leave for 1 minute, then drain. Plunge the tomatoes into cold water to cool, then peel off the skins. Quarter, remove the seeds and chop.

Heat the oil in a frying pan and cook the onion gently for 10 minutes until softened. Add the garlic, chopped tomatoes and sugar. Gently cook for 10 minutes until thickened. Remove from the heat and stir the rice, nuts and oregano into the sauce. Season to taste with salt and pepper.

Halve the peppers lengthways, cutting through and leaving the stem on. Remove the seeds and cores, then put the peppers in a lightly oiled roasting tin, cut-side down, and cook in the preheated oven for about 10 minutes. Turn the peppers so they are cut-side up. Spoon in the filling, then cover with kitchen foil. Return to the oven for 15 minutes, or until the peppers are very tender, removing the foil for the last 5 minutes to allow the tops to brown a little. Serve with a mixed salad and crusty bread.

Remaining peppers will keep well in the refrigerator for up to 2 days, but will not freeze well. Place in a dish and cover with clingfilm. Eat hot or cold. To reheat, pierce the clingfilm and microwave on High for 2 minutes, allow to stand for 1 minute. Or, heat the oven to 180°C/350°F/Gas Mark 4. Place the peppers in an ovenproof dish, pour a little water around the base. Cover with kitchen foil and heat for 15–20 minutes until piping hot.

Baby Onion Risotto

Makes 2 Portions

For the baby onions:

1 tbsp vegetable or olive oil
175 g/6 oz baby onions, peeled
and halved if large
pinch of sugar
1 tsp freshly chopped thyme

For the risotto:

1 tbsp vegetable or olive oil
1 small onion, peeled and
finely chopped
2 garlic cloves, peeled and
finely chopped
175 g/6 oz risotto rice
600 ml/1 pint hot vegetable stock
50 g/2 oz low-fat soft goat's cheese
salt and freshly ground black pepper
fresh thyme sprigs, to garnish
rocket leaves, to serve (optional)

For the onions, heat the oil in a saucepan and add the onions and sugar. Cover and cook over a low heat, stirring occasionally, for 20–25 minutes until caramelised. Uncover during the last 10 minutes. Meanwhile, for the risotto, heat the oil in a large frying pan and add the chopped onion. Cook over a medium heat for 5 minutes until softened. Add the garlic and cook for a further 30 seconds. Add the rice and stir well. Add the stock a ladleful at a time, stirring well and waiting until the last ladleful has been absorbed before stirring in the next. It will take 20–25 minutes to add all the stock; the rice should be just cooked but still firm. Remove from the heat.

Add the thyme to the onions and cook briefly. Increase the heat and allow the mixture to bubble for 2–3 minutes until almost evaporated. Add the onions to the risotto along with the goat's cheese. Stir well and season to taste with salt and pepper. Garnish with sprigs of fresh thyme. Serve immediately with the rocket leaves, if using.

This will keep well in the refrigerator for up to 2 days. Spoon into a dish and cover with clingfilm. I would not recommend freezing. To reheat, place in a saucepan over a gentle heat, add a little extra stock, bring slowly to the boil and simmer for 5–8 minutes, stirring occasionally, until piping hot. Or, reheat in the microwave. Spoon into a microwaveable dish or plate, cover with clingfilm, pierce 2–3 times and heat on High for 2 minutes. Allow to stand for 1 minute before eating.

Aduki Bean & Rice Burgers

Makes 2 portions

2 tbsp vegetable or sunflower oil
1 small onion, peeled and very
finely chopped
1 garlic clove, peeled and crushed
1 tsp curry paste
125 g/4 oz basmati rice
200 g/7 oz canned aduki beans,
drained and rinsed
125 ml/4 fl oz vegetable stock
50 g/2 oz firm tofu, crumbled
1 tbsp freshly chopped coriander
salt and freshly ground black pepper

For the carrot raita:

1 small carrot, peeled and grated
1/4 cucumber, cut into tiny dice
50 ml/2 fl oz Greek yogurt

To serve:

wholemeal baps
tomato slices
lettuce leaves

Heat 1 tablespoon of the oil in a saucepan and gently cook the onion for 5–8 minutes until soft. Add the garlic and curry paste and cook for a few more seconds. Stir in the rice and beans. Pour in the stock, bring to the boil and simmer for 12 minutes, or until all the stock has been absorbed – do not lift the lid for the first 10 minutes of cooking. Reserve.

Lightly mash the tofu. Add to the rice mixture with the coriander, salt and pepper. Mix. Divide the mixture into 4 and shape into burgers. Chill in the refrigerator for 30 minutes. Meanwhile, make the raita. Mix together the carrot, cucumber and Greek yogurt. Spoon into a small bowl and chill in the refrigerator until ready to serve.

Heat the remaining oil in a large frying pan. Fry the burgers for 4–5 minutes on each side, or until lightly browned. Serve in the baps with tomato slices and lettuce. Accompany with the raita.

If wishing to eat two of the burgers the next day, shape but do not fry. Place on a plate, cover with clingfilm and refrigerate. They will also feeze, if liked. Wrap in kitchen foil, label and date. Keep for up to 1 month. Thaw before cooking. In either case, cook as above when required.

Sausage & Bacon Risotto

Makes 1 large portion

75 g/3 oz long-grain rice
1 tsp olive or vegetable oil
25 g/1 oz butter, margarine or
1 tablespoon oil
125 g/4 oz cocktail sausages
1 shallot, peeled and finely chopped
25 g/1 oz bacon lardons or thick
slices of streaky bacon, chopped
50 g/2 oz chorizo or similar spicy
sausage, cut into chunks
$1/2$ green pepper, deseeded and
cut into strips
75 g canned sweetcorn, drained
1 tbsp freshly chopped parsley
25 g/1 oz mozzarella cheese, grated

Cook the rice in a saucepan of boiling salted water for 15 minutes or until tender, or according to packet instructions. Drain and rinse in cold water. Drain again and leave until completely cold.

Meanwhile, heat the wok or large frying pan, pour in the oil and melt the butter, margarine or add the extra oil, if using. Cook the cocktail sausages, turning continuously until cooked. Remove with a slotted spoon, cut in half and keep warm. Add the chopped shallot and bacon to the wok or frying pan and cook for 2–3 minutes until cooked but not browned. Add the spicy sausage and green pepper and stir-fry for a further 3 minutes. Add the cold rice and the sweetcorn to the wok or frying pan and stir-fry for 2 minutes, then return the cooked sausages to the wok or frying pan and stir over the heat until everything is piping hot. Garnish with the freshly chopped parsley and serve immediately with a little grated mozzarella cheese.

Leftovers will keep well in the refrigerator for up to 2 days. Spoon into a clean dish or bowl and cover with clingfilm. It will also freeze well. Place in a freezer bag, label and date. Keep for up to 1 month. Thaw in the refrigerator overnight. To reheat, stir the risotto and cover with clean clingfilm. Heat on High for 2 minutes, then allow to stand for 1 minute. Check it is piping hot; if not, reheat for an extra minute. Or, the risotto can be reheated in a saucepan. Pour a little oil into the pan, heat, then add the risotto. Cook over a gentle heat for 8–10 minutes, stirring frequently. Add a little water or stock if beginning to stick. Heat until piping hot.

Hearty Meals

Sometimes you just want something you can tuck into, something that will fill your belly and warm your cockles. Well, in this chapter we've got a tempting array of hearty, traditional fare and some slightly more original dishes. We show you how to make the best-ever sausage and mash and a wonderfully comforting Shepherd's Pie. If you're feeling more cosmopolitan, how about Ratatouille or Cassoulet?

Chilli Con Carne with Crispy-skinned Potato

Makes 1 large portion

1 tbsp vegetable or sunflower oil, plus extra for brushing

1 small onion, peeled and finely chopped

1 garlic clove, peeled and finely chopped

1/2–1 red chilli, deseeded and finely chopped (optional)

175 g/6 oz lean beef mince

1–2 tsp, depending on heat tolerance, chilli powder

200 g/7 oz canned tomatoes, chopped

2 tsp tomato purée

100 g/3 1/2 oz canned red kidney beans, drained and rinsed

1 large baking potato

coarse salt and freshly ground black pepper

To serve:

ready-made guacamole (optional)

Greek yogurt or natural yogurt

Preheat the oven to 150°C/300°F/Gas Mark 2. Heat the oil in a flameproof casserole and add the onion. Cook gently for 5–8 minutes until soft and lightly browned. Add the garlic and chilli, if using, and cook briefly. Increase the heat. Add the lean mince and cook for a further 5 minutes, stirring occasionally, until browned. Add the chilli powder and stir well. Cook for about 2 minutes, then add the chopped tomatoes and tomato purée. Bring slowly to the boil. Cover and cook in the preheated oven for 1 1/2 hours. Remove from the oven and stir in the kidney beans. Return to the oven for a further 15 minutes. Meanwhile, brush a little vegetable oil all over the potato and rub on some coarse salt. Put the potato in the oven alongside the chilli.

Remove the chilli and potato from the oven. Cut a cross in the potato, and then squeeze to open slightly and season to taste with salt and pepper. Serve with the chilli, guacamole and yogurt.

Keep any remaining cooked chilli in a clean bowl covered with clingfilm in the refrigerator for up to 2 days. Or, place in a freezer bag, label and date. Freeze for up to 2 weeks and thaw in the refrigerator for at least 8 hours. To reheat, spoon into a small saucepan, place over a gentle heat on the hob and cook, stirring, for 8–10 minutes, adding a little extra stock or water if looking dry. Or, heat in a small bowl covered with clingfilm and pierced 2–3 times on High in the microwave for 2 minutes. Stand for 1 minute, then stir before eating. Serve with freshly cooked rice.

Ratatouille

Makes 1 large portion

$^1/_2$ small red pepper
1 small courgette, trimmed
$^1/_4$ small aubergine, trimmed
1 small onion, peeled
2 small ripe tomatoes
25 g/1 oz button mushrooms, wiped
and halved or quartered
75 ml/3 fl oz tomato juice
1 tsp freshly chopped basil
salt and freshly ground
black pepper

Deseed the pepper if necessary; remove the membrane with a small sharp knife and cut into small dice. Thickly slice the courgette and cut the aubergine into small dice. Slice the onion into rings.

Place the tomatoes in boiling water until their skins begin to peel away. Remove the skins, cut the tomatoes into quarters and remove the seeds.

Place all the vegetables in a saucepan with the tomato juice and basil. Season to taste with salt and pepper. Bring to the boil, cover and simmer for 15 minutes or until the vegetables are tender. Remove the vegetables with a slotted spoon and arrange in a serving dish.

Bring the liquid in the pan to the boil and boil for 20 seconds until it is slightly thickened. Season the sauce to taste with salt and pepper. Pass the sauce through a sieve to remove some of the seeds and pour over the vegetables. Serve the ratatouille hot or cold.

Spoon any remaining ratatouille into a small bowl and cover with clingfilm. Keep in the refrigerator for up to 2 days. Do not freeze. The ratatouille can be reheated or eaten cold. If eating hot, spoon the ratatouille and its liquid into a small saucepan. Place over a gentle heat and bring to just below boiling point. Reduce the heat to a simmer and continue to heat for 5 minutes or until piping hot. Stir occasionally, adding a little extra tomato juice or water if becoming dry.

Pork Sausages with Onion Gravy & Best-ever Mash

Makes 2 large portions

1 tbsp vegetable or olive oil
1 medium onion, peeled
and thinly sliced
pinch sugar
1 tsp freshly chopped thyme or use
$1/2$ tsp dried thyme
1 tsp plain flour
150 ml/$1/4$ pint vegetable stock
6 pork sausages

For the mash:

225 g/8 oz floury potatoes, peeled
2 tsp margarine or butter
2 tbsp natural yogurt or milk
salt and freshly ground
black pepper

Heat the oil and add the onion. Cover and cook gently for about 12 minutes until the onion has collapsed. Add the sugar and stir well. Uncover and continue to cook, stirring often, until the onion is very soft and golden. Add the thyme, stir well, then add the flour, stirring. Gradually add the stock. Bring to the boil and simmer gently for 10 minutes.

Meanwhile, put the sausages in a frying pan and cook over a medium heat for about 15–20 minutes, turning often, until golden brown and slightly sticky all over.

For the mash, boil the potatoes in plenty of lightly salted water for 15–18 minutes until tender. Drain well and return to the saucepan. Put the saucepan over a low heat to allow the potatoes to dry thoroughly. Remove from the heat and add the margarine or butter, yogurt or milk and salt and pepper. Mash thoroughly. Serve the potato mash with the sausages and onion gravy.

Place any remaining sausages and mash on a plate, cover with clingfilm and keep overnight in the refrigerator. Pour any gravy into a small jug and cover with clingfilm. Do not freeze. To reheat, pierce the clingfilm covering the sausages and mash in 2–3 places. Microwave on High for 2 minutes 20 seconds. Allow to stand for 1 minute. If not piping hot, heat for a further minute. Stand for 1 more minute then eat. Pour the gravy into a small pan and heat, stirring until it comes to the boil. Add a little extra stock if needed.

Black Bean Chilli

Makes 1 large portion

75 g/3 oz black beans and black-eye
beans, soaked overnight
1 tbsp vegetable or olive oil
1 small onion, peeled and
finely chopped
1/2 red pepper, deseeded and diced
1 garlic clove, peeled and
finely chopped
1/2–1 red chilli, deseeded and finely
chopped (optional)
1 tsp chilli powder
1/2 tsp ground cumin
1 tsp ground coriander
150 g/5 oz canned tomatoes,
chopped
300 ml/1/2 pint vegetable stock
salt and freshly ground black pepper

To serve:

chunky guacamole or avocado salsa
(optional)
low-fat natural yogurt
lime or lemon slices (optional)
coriander sprigs

Drain the beans and place in a medium saucepan with at least twice their volume of fresh water. Bring slowly to the boil, skimming off any froth that rises to the surface. Boil rapidly for 10 minutes, then reduce the heat and simmer for about 45 minutes, adding more water if necessary. Drain and reserve.

Heat the oil in a medium saucepan and add the onion and pepper. Cook for 3–4 minutes until softened. Add the garlic and chilli, if using. Cook for 5 minutes, or until the onion and pepper have softened. Add the chilli powder, cumin and coriander and cook for 30 seconds. Add the beans along with the canned tomatoes, stock and seasoning to taste. Bring to the boil and simmer uncovered for 40–45 minutes until the beans and vegetables are tender and the sauce has reduced. Stir occasionally and add a little extra stock if becoming too dry. Remove the chilli from the heat. Leave for 2 minutes. Stir well. Serve with the chunky guacamole or avocado salsa, if using, yogurt, lemon or lime wedges, if using, and coriander.

The chilli will intensify with keeping. Place any remaining in a bowl and cover with clingfilm. Keep in the refrigerator for up to 3 days. If liked, it can be frozen. Spoon into a container or freezer bag, label and date. Keep for up to 1 month. Thaw in the refrigerator. Reheat in a pan over a gentle heat for 10–12 minutes. Add a little extra stock or water and stir occasionally.

Chargrilled Vegetable & Goats' Cheese Pizza

Makes 1 large portion

1 bought 23–30 cm/10–12 inch
pizza base

For the topping:

1 small aubergine,
thinly sliced
1 small courgette trimmed and
sliced lengthways
1/2 yellow pepper, deseeded
and cut in half
1 small red onion, peeled and
sliced into very thin wedges
2 tbsp vegetable or olive oil
50 g/2 oz cooked new
potatoes, halved
200 g/7 oz canned tomatoes,
chopped and drained
1 tsp freshly chopped oregano
50 g/2 oz goats' cheese, crumbled

Preheat the oven to 220°C/425°F/Gas Mark 7, 15 minutes before using. Put a baking sheet in the oven to heat up, 5 minutes before baking the pizza. Line a grill rack with kitchen foil.

To make the topping, arrange the aubergine, courgette, pepper and onion, skin-side up, on the grill rack and brush with 1 tablespoon of the oil. Grill for 4–5 minutes. Turn the vegetables and brush with the remaining oil. Grill for 3–4 minutes. Cool, skin and slice the pepper.

Put all of the vegetables in a bowl, add the halved new potatoes and toss gently together. Set aside.

Mix the tomatoes and oregano together and spread over the pizza base. Put the pizza on the preheated baking sheet and bake for 8 minutes.

Arrange the vegetables and goats' cheese on top and bake for 8–10 minutes. Serve.

The pizza needs to be eaten immediately and does not keep successfully.

Vegetable & Lentil Casserole

Makes 1 large portion

125 g/4 oz puy lentils
1–2 tbsp vegetable or olive oil
1 small onion, peeled and chopped
2 garlic cloves, peeled and crushed
150 g/5 oz carrots, peeled and
sliced into chunks
1 celery stalk, trimmed and sliced
175 g/6 oz butternut squash, peeled,
seeds removed and diced
450 ml/³/₄ pint vegetable stock
salt and freshly ground
black pepper
few fresh oregano sprigs,
plus extra to garnish
1 small red pepper,
deseeded and chopped
1 small courgette, trimmed
and sliced
2–3 tbsp natural yogurt or sour
cream, to serve

Preheat the oven to 160°C/325°F/Gas Mark 3. Pour the lentils out onto a plate and look through them for any small stones, then rinse the lentils and reserve. Heat the oil in a large ovenproof casserole (or a deep frying pan); add the onion, garlic, carrots and celery and sauté for 5 minutes, stirring occasionally. Add the squash and lentils. Pour in the stock and season to taste with salt and pepper. Add the oregano sprigs and bring to the boil.

If a frying pan has been used, transfer everything to a casserole. Cover with a lid and cook in the oven for 25 minutes. Remove from the oven; add the red pepper and courgette and stir. Return the casserole to the oven and cook for a further 20 minutes, or until all the vegetables are tender. Adjust the seasoning, garnish with oregano sprigs and serve with sour cream on the side.

This will keep well in the refrigerator for up to 3 days. Spoon any remaining casserole into a dish and cover with clingfilm. To reheat, place in an ovenproof dish and add a little extra stock if looking a little dry. Cover with kitchen foil and heat at 180°C/350°F/Gas Mark 4 for 20 minutes or until piping hot. Stir once or twice during reheating. Or, reheat in the microwave. Place the casserole in a microwavable dish and cover with clingfilm. Pierce the film 2–3 times. Heat on High for 3 minutes then stir and allow to stand for 1 minute before eating.

Roasted Butternut Squash

ℰ

Makes 2 large portions

1 small butternut squash
2 garlic cloves, peeled and crushed
2 tbsp vegetable or olive oil
salt and freshly ground black pepper
1 medium-sized leek, trimmed,
cleaned and thinly sliced
200 g/7 oz canned cannellini beans,
drained and rinsed
25 g/1 oz fine French beans, halved
150 ml/$\frac{1}{4}$ pint vegetable stock
25 g/1 oz rocket or watercress
2 tsp freshly snipped chives
fresh chives, to garnish (optional)

To serve:

4 tbsp natural or Greek yogurt
mixed salad

Preheat the oven to 200°C/400°F/Gas Mark 6. Cut the butternut squash in half lengthwise and scoop out all of the seeds. Score the squash in a diamond pattern with a sharp knife. Mix the garlic with one tablespoon of the oil and brush over the cut surfaces of the squash. Season well with salt and pepper. Put on a baking sheet and roast for 40 minutes until tender.

Heat the remaining oil in a saucepan and fry the leeks for 5 minutes. Add the drained cannellini beans, French beans and vegetable stock. Bring to the boil and simmer gently for 5 minutes until the French beans are tender. Remove from the heat and stir in the rocket or watercress and chives. Season well. Remove the squash from the oven and allow to cool for 5 minutes. Spoon in the bean mixture. Garnish with a few snipped chives, if using, and serve immediately with the yogurt and a mixed salad.

The squash will keep well in the refrigerator for up to 2 days. Place on a plate and cover with clingfilm. I would not recommend freezing. To reheat, place the squash in a roasting tin and pour round a little water. Cover with kitchen foil and reheat in an oven preheated to 180°C/350°F/Gas Mark 4 for 15–20 minutes until piping hot. Or, it can be reheated in the microwave. Place on a microwaveable dish or plate and cover with clingfilm. Pierce 2–3 times, heat on High for 2 minutes 30 seconds and allow to stand for 1 minute before eating.

Tuna Mushroom Ragout

Makes 2 large portions

125 g/4 oz basmati and wild rice
25 g/1 oz margarine or butter
1 tbsp vegetable or olive oil
1 small onion, peeled and
finely chopped
1 garlic clove, peeled and crushed
150 g/5 oz button mushrooms,
wiped and halved
1 tbsp plain flour
200 g/7 oz canned tomatoes,
chopped
1 tsp freshly chopped parsley
dash of Worcestershire sauce
(optional)
200 g can tuna in oil, drained
salt and freshly ground black pepper
2 tbsp Parmesan or
Cheddar cheese, grated
1 tsp freshly shredded basil

To serve:

green salad and garlic bread

Cook the basmati and wild rice in a saucepan of boiling salted water for 20 minutes, then drain and return to the pan. Stir in half of the margarine or butter, cover the pan and leave to stand for 2 minutes until all of the margarine or butter has melted.

Heat the oil and the remaining margarine or butter in a frying pan and cook the onion for 1–2 minutes until soft. Add the garlic and mushrooms and continue to cook for a further 3 minutes. Stir in the flour and cook for 1 minute, then add the canned tomatoes with their juice and bring the sauce to the boil. Add the parsley, Worcestershire sauce, if using, and tuna and simmer gently for 3 minutes. Season to taste with salt and freshly ground pepper.

Stir the rice well, place on two plates and spoon the tuna and mushroom mixture on top of the rice. Sprinkle with the grated cheese and the basil. Serve immediately with a green salad and chunks of garlic bread, if liked.

Any remaining ragout and rice can be placed on a clean plate, covered with clingfilm and left overnight in the refrigerator. Do not freeze. The next day, the ragout could be eaten cold as a salad. If you'd like it hot, cover with clean clingfilm, pierce 2–3 times, and heat on High in the microwave for 2 minutes. Allow to stand for 1 minute before eating.

Egg & Bacon Pie

Cuts into 4–6 portions

225 g/8 oz bought shortcrust pastry
flour, for dusting

For the filling:

40 g/1½ oz margarine or butter
40 g/1½ oz plain white flour
450 ml/¾ pint milk, warmed
225 g/8 oz back bacon rashers,
trimmed of fat and cut into
small strips
salt and freshly ground
black pepper
3 medium eggs, plus egg
for brushing
chips and baked tomatoes,
to serve

Preheat the oven to 200°C/400°F/Gas Mark 6, 15 minutes before required. Cut the pastry in half. Roll out on a lightly floured surface and use one half to line a deep 20.5 cm/8 inch pie dish. Melt the fat in a small pan and sprinkle in the flour. Stir over a medium heat for 2 minutes, until thickened (it will form a slightly grainy paste). Draw off the heat and gradually stir in the warmed milk. Return to the heat, stirring constantly, until the mixture is thick enough to coat the back of a wooden spoon. Remove from the heat, add the bacon a little at a time, and stir. Season to taste and leave to cool.

Beat the eggs and then stir them into the cooled sauce. Spoon the mixture into the pastry-lined dish. Roll the remaining pastry out to form a pie lid. Lightly brush the pastry on the edge of the dish with egg or cold water. Wrap the pastry lid around the rolling pin and place in position over the pie dish. Press the edges together firmly and trim. Make a decorative edge round the pie. Brush the top of the pie with beaten egg and cut slits across the top to allow the steam to escape. Place on a baking sheet and bake in the preheated oven. After 15 minutes, reduce the oven temperature to 180°C/350°F/Gas Mark 4. Brush the top of the pie again with the beaten egg. Continue to bake for a further 20–25 minutes until the pie is golden and the filling has set. Serve warm or cold with chips and baked tomatoes.

This pie will keep for 3–4 days in the refrigerator. It is good eaten cold. Once cool, cover the top with clingfilm and keep in the refrigerator. I would not recommend freezing or reheating.

Shepherd's Pie

Makes 3 large portions

1 tbsp vegetable or olive oil
1 onion, peeled and finely chopped
1 carrot, peeled and finely chopped
1 celery stalk, trimmed and
finely chopped
450 g/1 lb fresh lean lamb mince
1 tbsp plain flour
2–3 sprigs of fresh thyme
150–200 ml/5–7 fl oz lamb or
vegetable stock
2 tbsp tomato purée
salt and freshly ground
black pepper
575 g/1¼ lb potatoes, peeled
and cut into chunks
1 tbsp margarine or butter
3–4 tbsp milk
1 tbsp freshly chopped parsley
fresh herbs, to garnish (optional)

Preheat the oven to 200°C/400°F/Gas Mark 6, about 15 minutes before cooking. Heat the oil in a large saucepan and add the onion, carrot and celery. Cook over a medium heat for 5 minutes, add the lamb and fry for a further 5 minutes, stirring, until the lamb has browned. Add the flour and cook for 2 minutes before adding the thyme, then stir in 150 ml/5 fl oz of the stock and the tomato purée. Season to taste and simmer gently for 10 minutes until reduced and thickened, adding a little more stock if needed (you want a moist, not wet, consistency). Remove from the heat to cool slightly and adjust seasoning if required.

Meanwhile, boil the potatoes in salted water for 12–15 minutes until tender. Drain and return to the pan over a low heat to dry out. Remove from the heat and add the margarine or butter, milk and parsley. Mash until creamy, adding more milk if necessary. Season. Transfer the lamb mixture to an ovenproof dish, spoon over the mash and spread evenly to cover. Fork the surface, place on a baking sheet and cook in the oven for 25–30 minutes until the top has browned and the filling is piping hot. Garnish and serve.

Spoon any remaining pie into containers. Once cool, cover with clingfilm or a lid. Keep for up to 2 days in the refrigerator, or label and date then freeze for up to 2 weeks. Thaw in the refrigerator overnight. To reheat, spoon a portion onto a plate, cover with clingfilm and pierce 2–3 times. Microwave on High for 2 minutes 20 seconds. Allow to stand for 1 minute, then, if not piping hot, reheat for a further minute.

Cassoulet

Makes 2 portions

1 tbsp vegetable or olive oil
1 onion, peeled and chopped
1 celery stalk, trimmed and chopped
2 carrots, peeled and sliced
2–3 garlic cloves, peeled
and crushed
225 g/8 oz pork belly (optional)
4 spicy thick sausages
few fresh thyme sprigs
salt and freshly ground
black pepper
400 g can cannellini beans,
drained and rinsed
600 ml/1 pint vegetable stock
50 g/2 oz fresh breadcrumbs
2 tbsp freshly chopped thyme

Preheat the oven to 180°C/350°F/Gas Mark 4. Heat the oil in a large saucepan or flameproof casserole, add the onion, celery, carrots and garlic and fry for 5 minutes. Cut the pork, if using, into small pieces and cut the sausages into chunks. Add the meat to the vegetables and cook, stirring, until lightly browned. Add the thyme sprigs and season to taste with salt and pepper. If a saucepan was used, transfer everything to an ovenproof casserole. Spoon the beans on top, then pour in the stock. Mix the breadcrumbs with 1 tablespoon of the chopped thyme in a small bowl and sprinkle on top of the beans. Cover with a lid and cook in the oven for 40 minutes. Remove the lid and cook for a further 15 minutes, or until the breadcrumbs are crisp. Sprinkle with the remaining chopped thyme and serve.

Any remaining cassoulet can be frozen. When cool, spoon into a container and cover with a lid. Label and date then freeze. Use within 2 weeks and thaw overnight in the refrigerator when required. Or, keep for up to 2–3 days in the refrigerator. Spoon the cassoulet into a dish and cover with clingfilm. To reheat, spoon into a clean dish and cover with clingfilm. Pierce 2–3 times. Heat on High for 2 minutes in the microwave, allow to stand for 1 minute and, if not piping hot, reheat for 1 minute, stand for a further minute, then eat. Alternatively, reheat on the hob. Spoon into a saucepan and heat gently. Bring to the boil, reduce to a simmer and heat for 8–10 minutes. Stir occasionally and, when piping hot, stir and eat.

Chicken Pie with Sweet Potato Topping

Makes 4 large portions

575g/1¼ lb sweet potatoes,
peeled and cut into chunks
salt and freshly ground
black pepper
4–5 tbsp milk
25 g/1 oz margarine or butter
2 tsp brown sugar
grated zest of 1 orange
450 g/1 lb boneless, skinless
chicken meat such as breast
1 medium onion, peeled
and coarsely chopped
125 g/4 oz button mushrooms,
stems trimmed
1 large leek, trimmed
and thickly sliced
150 ml/¼ pint water
1 chicken stock cube
1 tbsp freshly chopped parsley
50 ml/2 fl oz natural yogurt
green vegetables, to serve

Preheat the oven to 190°C/375°F/Gas Mark 5, 10 minutes before required. Cook the potatoes in lightly salted boiling water until tender. Drain well, then return to the saucepan and mash until smooth and creamy, gradually adding the milk, then the margarine or butter, sugar and orange zest. Season to taste with salt and pepper and reserve.

Place the chicken in a saucepan with the onion, mushrooms, leek, water and stock cube and season to taste. Simmer, covered for 20 minutes, until the vegetables are tender. Using a slotted spoon, transfer the chicken and vegetables to a 1.1 litre/2 pint pie dish. Add the parsley and yogurt to the liquid in the pan and bring to the boil. Simmer until thickened and smooth, stirring constantly. Pour over the chicken in the pie dish, mix and cool.

Spread the mashed sweet potato over the chicken filling, and swirl the surface into decorative peaks. Bake in the preheated oven for 35 minutes, or until the top is golden and the chicken filling is piping hot. Serve immediately with fresh green vegetables.

Keep any remaining pie in lidded containers or on a plate covered with clingfilm in the refrigerator for up to 2 days or freeze for up to 2 weeks. If freezing, label and date and thaw overnight in the refrigerator. Reheat in a clean dish, covered with clingfilm and pierced 2–3 times, in the microwave on High for 2 minutes 30 seconds. Stand for 1 minute. If not piping hot, heat for an extra minute.

Braised Chicken in Beer

Makes 2 large portions

2 chicken joints, skinned
50 g/2 oz pitted dried prunes
(optional)
2 bay leaves
4 small onions
2 tsp vegetable or olive oil
75 g/3 oz small button
mushrooms, wiped
1 tsp soft dark brown sugar
$^1/_2$–1 tsp whole-grain mustard
2 tsp tomato purée
150 ml/$^1/_4$ pint light ale
150 ml/$^1/_4$ pint chicken stock
salt and freshly ground
black pepper
2 tsp cornflour
2 tsp lemon juice
2 tbsp chopped fresh parsley
flat-leaf parsley, to garnish (optional)

To serve:

mashed potatoes
seasonal green vegetables

Preheat the oven to 190°C/ 375°F/Gas Mark 5. Cut each chicken joint in half and put in an ovenproof casserole with the prunes and bay leaves. Cover the onions with boiling water. Drain after 2 minutes and rinse under cold water. The skins should then peel away easily.

Heat the oil in a frying pan. Add the onions and gently cook for about 5 minutes until beginning to colour. Add the mushrooms and cook for a further 3–4 minutes until both the mushrooms and onions are softened. Sprinkle over the sugar, then add the mustard, tomato purée, ale and stock. Season to taste with salt and pepper and bring to the boil, stirring to combine. Carefully pour over the chicken. Cover and cook in the preheated oven for 45 minutes. Blend the cornflour with the lemon juice and 1 tablespoon of cold water and stir into the chicken casserole. Return the casserole to the oven for a further 10 minutes or until the chicken is cooked and the vegetables are tender. Remove the bay leaves and stir in the chopped parsley. Garnish the chicken with the flat-leaf parsley, if using. Serve with the mash and green vegetables.

Spoon leftover chicken into a container, cover with a lid, label and date. Either refrigerate for up to 2 days or freeze for up to 1 month. If frozen, allow to thaw overnight in the refrigerator. Reheat in a dish or on a plate, covered with clingfilm and pierced 2–3 times, on High in the microwave for 2 minutes 30 seconds. Allow to stand for 1 minute. If not piping hot, heat for a further minute.

Cheesy Chicken Burgers

Makes 2 small burgers

1 tbsp sunflower oil
1 small onion, peeled and chopped
1 garlic clove, peeled and crushed
$1/4$ red pepper, deseeded
and finely chopped
175 g/6 oz fresh chicken mince
1 tbsp 0%-fat Greek yogurt
2 tbsp fresh breadcrumbs
1 tsp freshly chopped herbs, such as
parsley or tarragon
15 g/$^1/_2$ oz Cheshire cheese, crumbled
salt and freshly ground black pepper

For the sweetcorn and carrot relish (optional):

50 g/2 oz canned sweetcorn, drained;
1 small carrot, peeled, grated;
$^1/_2$ green chilli, deseeded and finely
chopped; 1 tsp vinegar or lemon
juice; 1 tsp light soft brown sugar

To serve:

wholemeal or granary rolls; lettuce;
sliced tomatoes; mixed salad leaves

Heat the oil in a frying pan and gently cook the onion and garlic for 5 minutes. Add the red pepper and cook for 5 minutes. Transfer into a bowl. Add the chicken, yogurt, breadcrumbs, herbs and cheese and season to taste with salt and pepper. Mix well. Divide the mixture equally into 2 and shape into burgers. Cover and chill for at least 20 minutes.

Put all the relish ingredients in a small saucepan with 1 tablespoon water and heat gently, stirring occasionally until all the sugar has dissolved. Cover and cook over a low heat for 2 minutes, then uncover and cook for a further minute, or until the relish is thick.

Preheat the grill to medium. Place the burgers on a lightly oiled grill pan and grill for 8–10 minutes on each side, or until browned and completely cooked through. Warm the rolls if liked, then split and fill with the burgers, lettuce, tomatoes and relish. Serve immediately with the salad leaves.

Prepared but uncooked burgers can be refrigerated for up to 2 days on a clean plate covered with clingfilm. Or, providing that the mince has not been previously frozen, open freeze on a plate for 3–4 hours until solid, wrap in kitchen foil, label and date. Thaw overnight in the fridge.

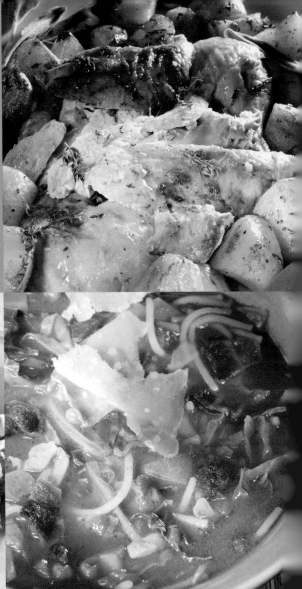

Impress
Your Friends

You won't always be cooking for one – with your newfound cooking skills it's inevitable that friends will be clamouring to be fed by you, and you might even manage some sophisticated 'dinner parties'. Not to mention – it would be great to surprise your parents when they come to visit. The delicious suggestions in this chapter are great to try when you're cooking for more than one as they don't store so well and may take a little longer to prepare.

Classic Minestrone

Makes 6–8 portions

25 g/1 oz butter or margarine
3 tbsp vegetable or olive oil
3 rashers streaky bacon
1 large onion, peeled
1 garlic clove, peeled
1 celery stalk, trimmed
2 carrots, peeled
400 g can tomatoes, chopped
1.1 litre/2 pints chicken stock
125 g/4 oz green cabbage,
finely shredded
50 g/2 oz French beans, trimmed
and halved
3 tbsp frozen peas
50 g/2 oz spaghetti, broken into
short pieces
salt and freshly ground
black pepper
Parmesan cheese shavings,
to garnish
crusty bread, to serve

Heat the butter or margarine and oil together in a large saucepan. Chop the bacon and add to the saucepan. Cook for 3–4 minutes, and then remove with a slotted spoon and reserve.

Finely chop the onion, garlic, celery and carrots and add to the saucepan, one ingredient at a time, stirring well after each addition. Cover and cook gently for 8–10 minutes until the vegetables are softened. Add the chopped tomatoes, with their juice and the stock, bring to the boil then cover the saucepan with a lid, reduce the heat and simmer gently for about 20 minutes. Stir in the cabbage, beans, peas and spaghetti pieces. Cover and simmer for a further 20 minutes, or until all the ingredients are tender. Season to taste with salt and pepper.

Return the cooked bacon to the saucepan and bring the soup to the boil. Serve the soup immediately with Parmesan cheese shavings sprinkled on the top and plenty of crusty bread to accompany it.

Any remaining minestrone will not freeze, but will keep well overnight in the refrigerator. Pour into a clean bowl and, when cool, cover with clingfilm and refrigerate. When ready to reheat, pour into a saucepan and place over a gentle heat. Heat for 8–10 minutes until piping hot.

Creamy Turkey & Tomato Pasta

Makes 4 portions

3 tbsp vegetable or olive oil
350 g/12 oz turkey breasts, cut into
bite-sized pieces
275 g/10 oz cherry tomatoes
2 garlic cloves, peeled
and chopped
3 tbsp vinegar, such as
malt or balsamic
salt and freshly ground
black pepper
350 g/12 oz tagliatelle
2 tbsp freshly chopped basil
200 ml tub crème fraîche or
natural yogurt
shaved Parmesan or mature
Cheddar cheese, to garnish

Preheat the oven to 200°C/400°F/Gas Mark 6. Heat 2 tablespoons of oil in a large frying pan. Add the turkey and cook for 5 minutes, or until sealed, turning occasionally. Transfer to a roasting tin and add the remaining oil, the tomatoes, garlic and vinegar. Stir well and season to taste. Roast for 30 minutes, or until the turkey is tender, turning the food once.

Meanwhile, bring a large pan of lightly salted water to a rolling boil. Add the pasta and cook according to the packet instructions, or until *al dente*. Drain, return to the pan and keep warm.

Stir the basil and seasoning into the crème fraîche or yogurt. Remove the tin from the oven. Stir the crème fraîche or yogurt mix into the turkey and tomatoes and return to the oven for 1–2 minutes, until piping hot. Stir the mixture into the pasta and toss lightly together. Tip into a warmed serving dish. Garnish with Parmesan cheese shavings and serve immediately.

This dish does not freeze well, but will keep in the refrigerator overnight. Once cool, spoon into a bowl, cover with clingfilm and place in the refrigerator. To reheat, pierce the clingfilm and microwave on High for 2 minutes. Remove and allow to stand for 1 minute. Stir, adding a little yogurt or water if too dry. If the pasta and turkey are not piping hot, return to the microwave for a further minute. The pasta can also be reheated in a pan on the hob. Spoon into a pan with 1–2 tablespoons water. Heat over a medium heat, stirring frequently for 8–10 minutes until piping hot.

Chicken with Mushrooms & Cream

Makes 4 portions

2 tbsp vegetable or olive oil
4 boneless chicken breasts,
preferably free range
2 garlic cloves, peeled and crushed
150 ml/1/4 pint white wine
or chicken stock
salt and freshly ground black pepper
25 g/1 oz butter or margarine
350 g/12 oz mushrooms, such as
large field or porcini, cleaned and
thickly sliced
125 ml/4 fl oz cream,
double or single
1 tbsp freshly chopped oregano
sprigs of fresh basil, to garnish
(optional)
freshly cooked rice, to serve

Heat the olive oil in a large, heavy-based frying pan, then add the chicken breasts, skin-side down and cook for about 5–8 minutes, until browned. Remove the chicken breasts and reserve. Add the garlic, stir into the juices and cook for 1 minute. Pour the white wine or stock into the pan and season to taste with salt and pepper. Return the chicken to the pan. Bring to the boil, reduce the heat to low and simmer for about 20 minutes, or until tender.

In another large frying pan, heat the butter and add the sliced mushrooms. Fry for 5 minutes, or until the mushrooms are golden and tender. Add the mushrooms and any juices to the chicken. Stir in the cream, season to taste, then add the chopped oregano. Stir together gently and cook for 2–3 minutes longer. Transfer to a large serving plate and garnish with sprigs of fresh basil, if desired. Serve immediately with rice.

The chicken and sauce in this recipe will not freeze, but are fine if kept in the refrigerator overnight. Place, once cool, in a dish and cover with clingfilm. To reheat, pierce the clingfilm in 2–3 places and heat on High in the microwave for 2 minutes 30 seconds. Allow to stand for 1 minute then stir. If not piping hot, heat for a further minute. If preferred, reheat in a nonstick saucepan. Spoon into the pan and bring to the boil, stirring. Lower the heat to a simmer and cover with a lid. Continue to simmer for 8–10 minutes until the chicken is piping hot. Stir occasionally.

Leek & Ham Risotto

Makes 4 portions

1 tbsp vegetable or olive oil
25 g/1 oz butter or margarine
1 medium onion, peeled
and finely chopped
4 leeks, trimmed and thinly sliced
1$^1/_2$ tbsp freshly chopped thyme or
use 1 tsp dried thyme
350 g/12 oz arborio rice
1.25 litres/2$^1/_4$ pints vegetable or
chicken stock, heated
225 g/8 oz cooked ham
175 g/6 oz peas, thawed if frozen
50 g/2 oz Parmesan or Cheddar
cheese, grated
salt and freshly ground
black pepper

Heat the oil and half the butter or margarine together in a large saucepan. Add the onion and leeks and cook over a medium heat for 6–8 minutes, stirring occasionally, until soft and beginning to colour. Stir in the thyme and cook briefly. Add the rice and stir well. Continue stirring over a medium heat for about 1 minute until the rice is glossy. Add a ladleful or two of the stock and stir well until the stock is absorbed. Continue adding stock, a ladleful at a time, and stirring well between additions, until about two-thirds of the stock has been added.

Meanwhile, either chop or finely shred the ham, then add to the saucepan of rice together with the peas. Continue adding ladlefuls of stock, as described above, until the rice is creamy and tender but with just a slight bite to it and the ham is heated thoroughly. You do not have to add all of the liquid. Add the remaining butter or margarine, sprinkle over the cheese and season to taste with salt and pepper. When the butter or margarine has melted and the cheese has softened, stir well to incorporate. Taste and adjust the seasoning, then serve immediately.

Rice does not freeze well and incorrect handling can result in food poisoning. However, this dish will keep overnight in the refrigerator. Spoon into a dish and cover with clingfilm. To reheat, pierce the clingfilm in 2–3 places and heat on High for 2 minutes. Allow to stand for 1 minute then stir. If not piping hot, heat for a further minute. Or, heat the risotto gently in a pan with a little extra oil, stirring, until piping hot. If dry, add a little stock.

Slow Roast Chicken with Potatoes & Oregano

Makes 6 portions

1.4–1.8 kg/3–4 lb
oven-ready chicken
1 lemon, halved
1 onion, peeled and quartered
50 g/2 oz butter or margarine,
softened
salt and freshly ground
black pepper
1 kg/2¼ lb potatoes, peeled
and quartered
3–4 tbsp vegetable or olive oil
1 tbsp dried oregano, crumbled
1 tsp fresh thyme leaves
2 tbsp freshly chopped thyme
fresh sage leaves, to garnish

Preheat the oven to 200°C/400°F/Gas Mark 6. Rinse the chicken and dry well, inside and out, with kitchen paper. Rub with the lemon halves, and squeeze the juice over and into the cavity. Put the squeezed halves into the cavity with the quartered onion. Rub the butter or margarine over the chicken and season to taste. Place in a large roasting tin, breast-side down.

Toss the potatoes in the oil, season to taste and add the oregano and fresh thyme. Arrange the potatoes around the chicken and carefully pour 150 ml/ ¼ pint water into one end of the pan (not over the oil). Roast in the oven for 25 minutes. Reduce the temperature to 190°C/375°F/Gas Mark 5 and turn the chicken breast-side up. Turn the potatoes, sprinkle over half the fresh herbs and baste the chicken and potatoes with the juices. Continue roasting for 1 hour, or until the chicken is cooked, basting occasionally. If the liquid evaporates completely, add a little more water. The chicken is done when the juices run clear when the thigh is pierced with a skewer. Transfer the chicken to a carving board and rest for 5 minutes, covered with kitchen foil. Return the potatoes to the oven while the chicken is resting. Carve the chicken and arrange on a large serving dish. Arrange the potatoes around the chicken and drizzle over any juices. Sprinkle with the remaining herbs and serve.

Place any remaining chicken on a plate, cover with clingfilm or kitchen foil and store in the refrigerator for up to 2 days. Use in risottos, pasta sauces or salads. If reheating, ensure that the chicken is piping hot before eating.

Lemon Chicken with Potatoes, Rosemary & Olives

Makes 6 portions

12 skinless boneless chicken thighs
1 large lemon
125 ml/4 fl oz vegetable or olive oil
4–6 garlic cloves, peeled and sliced
2 onions, peeled and thinly sliced
4–6 fresh rosemary sprigs
1.1 kg/2^1/$_2$ lb potatoes,
peeled and cut into
4 cm/1^1/$_2$ inch pieces
salt and freshly ground black pepper
18–24 black olives, pitted (optional)
freshly cooked carrots
and courgettes, to serve

Preheat oven to 200˚C/400˚F/Gas Mark 6, 15 minutes before cooking. Trim the chicken thighs and place in a shallow baking dish large enough to hold them in a single layer. Remove the zest from the lemon and cut into thin strips. Reserve half and add the remainder to the chicken. Squeeze the lemon juice over the chicken, toss to coat well and leave to stand for 10 minutes.

Add the remaining lemon strips, oil, garlic, onions and half of the rosemary sprigs. Toss gently and leave for about 20 minutes.

Cover the potatoes with lightly salted water and bring to the boil. Cook for 2 minutes, then drain well and add to the chicken. Season to taste with salt and pepper.

Roast the chicken in the preheated oven for 50 minutes, turning frequently and basting, or until the chicken is cooked. Just before the end of cooking time, discard the rosemary, and add fresh sprigs of rosemary. Add the olives, if using, and stir. Serve immediately with the carrots and courgettes.

Any remaining chicken thighs can be cooled, placed on a clean plate and covered with kitchen foil. Keep in the refrigerator for up to 2 days. Do not reheat the chicken thighs on their own as they will be dry. Use when making pasta or rice dishes, as part of a topping for pizza or cold with salad.

Chicken & Summer Vegetable Risotto

Makes 4 portions

1 litre/1³/₄ pint chicken
or vegetable stock
125 g/4 oz baby asparagus spears
(optional)
175 g/6 oz French beans
15 g/¹/₂ oz butter or margarine
1 small onion, peeled
and finely chopped
275 g/10 oz arborio rice
¹/₂ tsp turmeric
75 g/3 oz frozen peas, thawed
225 g/8 oz cooked chicken,
skinned and diced
juice of ¹/₂ lemon
salt and freshly ground black pepper
25 g/1 oz Parmesan or Cheddar
cheese, shaved

Bring the stock to the boil in a large saucepan. Trim the asparagus, if using, and cut into 4 cm/1¹/₂ inch lengths. Blanch in the stock for 1–2 minutes until tender, remove with a slotted spoon and reserve. Halve the green beans and cook in the boiling stock for 4 minutes. Remove and reserve. Turn down the heat and keep the stock barely simmering.

Melt the butter or margarine in a heavy-based saucepan. Add the onion and cook gently for about 5 minutes. Add the rice and cook, stirring for 1 minute until the grains are coated and look translucent. Add the turmeric and a ladle of the stock. Simmer, stirring all the time, until the stock has absorbed. Continue adding the stock, a ladle at a time, waiting for it to absorb. After 15 minutes the risotto should be creamy with a slight bite to it. If not, add a little more stock and cook for a few more minutes, or until ready. Add the peas, reserved vegetables, chicken and lemon juice. Season to taste and cook for 3–4 minutes until the chicken is piping hot. Spoon the risotto on to warmed serving plates. Scatter each portion with a few shavings of Parmesan or Cheddar cheese and serve immediately.

Any remaining risotto will keep overnight in the refrigerator, spooned into a dish and covered with clingfilm. To reheat, pierce the clingfilm in 2–3 places and heat on High for 2 minutes. Allow to stand for 1 minute then stir. If not piping hot, heat for a further minute. Or, heat the risotto gently in a pan with a little extra oil, stirring, until piping hot. If becoming dry, add a little stock.

Pork Chop Hotpot

Makes 4 portions

4 pork chops
flour for dusting
225 g/8 oz shallots, peeled
2 garlic cloves, peeled
50 g/2 oz sun-dried tomatoes or
2 ripe fresh tomatoes
2 tbsp vegetable or olive oil
400 g can plum tomatoes
300 ml/1/2 pint chicken stock
2 tbsp tomato purée
2 tbsp freshly chopped oregano,
or 2 tsp dried
salt and freshly ground black pepper
fresh oregano leaves,
to garnish (optional)

To serve:

freshly cooked new potatoes
French beans

Preheat oven to 190°C/375°F/Gas Mark 5, 10 minutes before cooking. Trim the pork chops, removing any excess fat, wipe with a clean, damp cloth. Dust with a little flour and reserve. Cut the shallots in half if large. Chop the garlic and the sun-dried or fresh tomatoes. Heat the oil in a large flame-proof casserole dish and cook the pork for about 5 minutes, turning occasionally, until browned all over. Using a slotted spoon, lift out of the dish and reserve. Add the shallots and cook for 5 minutes, stirring. Return the pork to the dish and scatter with the garlic and sun-dried or fresh tomatoes, and then pour over the can of tomatoes with their juice.

Blend the stock and tomato purée together and add the oregano. Season to taste, then pour over the pork and bring to a gentle boil. Cover with a close-fitting lid and cook in the oven for 1 hour, or until the pork is tender. Adjust the seasoning to taste, scatter with a few oregano leaves, if using, and serve immediately with freshly cooked potatoes and beans.

Any remaining pork chops and sauce can be placed in a dish. Either label and date and freeze for up to 1 month or cover and refrigerate for up to 2 days. If frozen, allow to thaw overnight in the refrigerator before using. To reheat, place in a casserole dish in the oven at 180°C/350°F/Gas Mark 4 for 20 minutes, or until piping hot. Add a little extra stock if becoming too dry. Or, place in a heavy-based saucepan on the hob and bring to the boil. Reduce to a gentle simmer for 20 minutes, or until piping hot. Add a little extra stock if necessary.

Toad in the Hole

Makes 4 portions

8 large pork sausages
125 g/4 oz plain flour
pinch salt
2 medium eggs
225 ml/8 fl oz milk
1 tbsp sunflower or vegetable oil

To serve:

seasonal vegetables
English mustard

Preheat the oven to 220°C/425°F/Gas Mark 7, 15 minutes before required. Lightly prick the sausages and reserve.

Sieve the flour and salt into a mixing bowl and make a well in the centre. Drop the eggs into the well and then, using a wooden spoon, beat in the eggs, drawing the flour in from the sides of the bowl. Gradually add the milk and beat to form a smooth batter without any lumps. Allow to stand for 30 minutes.

When ready to cook, pour the oil into a 25.5 x 20.5 cm/10 x 8 inch roasting tin. Heat until almost smoking and then add the sausages. Carefully turn the sausages in the hot oil and return to the oven for 5 minutes.

Remove from the oven and turn them over again. Stir the batter well and pour over the sausages. Return to the oven and cook for 35–40 minutes until the pudding is well risen and golden brown. Serve immediately with seasonal vegetables and English mustard.

Toad in the hole does not freeze or keep well overnight in the refrigerator. You simply have to eat it all, so get your friends round!

Treats & Desserts

Once you've realized how easy it is to whip up tasty savoury meals, you will likely be itching to try your hand at some of these sweet treats. The cakes make great alternatives to presents for a friend's birthday, and the cookies are quick and easy – ideal for a pick-me up snack when the studying gets too dull. Or if you're missing home and it's a comforting dessert you're after, the Chocolate & Fruit Crumble is the perfect answer.

Chocolate Chip Cookies

Makes 18

75 g/3 oz plain flour
pinch of salt
$^1/_2$ tsp baking powder
40 g/1$^1/_2$ oz butter or margarine
50 g/2 oz soft light brown sugar
1$^1/_2$ tbsp golden syrup
50 g/2 oz chocolate chips

Preheat the oven to 190°C/375°F/Gas Mark 5, 10 minutes before baking. Lightly oil 1–2 large baking sheets.

In a large bowl, sift together the flour, salt and baking powder.

Cut the butter or margarine into small pieces and add to the flour mixture. Using 2 knives or the fingertips, rub in the butter or margarine until the mixture resembles coarse breadcrumbs. Add the light brown sugar, golden syrup and chocolate chips. Mix together until a smooth dough forms.

Shape the mixture into small balls and arrange on the baking sheet, leaving enough space to allow them to expand. (These cookies do not increase in size by a great deal, but allow a little space for expansion.) Flatten the mixture slightly with the fingertips or the heel of the hand.

Bake in the preheated oven for 12–15 minutes until golden and cooked through. Allow to cool slightly, and then transfer the biscuits onto a wire rack to cool. Serve when cold or otherwise store in an airtight tin.

Chocolate Fudge Brownies

Makes 16

125 g/4 oz butter or margarine
175 g/6 oz dark chocolate, roughly
chopped or broken
225 g/8 oz caster sugar
2 tsp vanilla extract
2 medium eggs, lightly beaten
150 g/5 oz plain flour

For the icing:

175 g/6 oz icing sugar
2 tbsp cocoa powder
15 g/$\frac{1}{2}$ oz butter or margarine

Preheat the oven to 180°C/350°F/Gas Mark 4, 10 minutes before baking. Lightly oil and line a 20.5 cm/8 inch square cake tin with greaseproof or baking paper.

Slowly melt the butter or margarine and chocolate together in a heatproof bowl placed over a saucepan of simmering water. Transfer the mixture to a large bowl. Stir in the sugar and vanilla extract, and then stir in the eggs. Sift over the flour and fold together well with a metal spoon or rubber spatula. Pour into the prepared tin.

Transfer to the preheated oven and bake for 30 minutes until just set. Remove the cooked mixture from the oven and leave to cool in the tin before turning it out on to a wire rack.

Sift the icing sugar and cocoa powder into a small bowl and make a well in the centre. Place the butter or margarine in the well then gradually add 1–2 tablespoons of hot water (when making icing, add the liquid a little at a time; this way you will be able to get the correct consistency). Mix to form a smooth spreadable icing.

Pour the icing over the cooked mixture. Allow the icing to set before cutting into squares. Serve the brownies when they are cold. Keep in an airtight tin for up to 1 week.

Classic Flapjacks

Makes 12

175 g/6 oz butter or margarine,
plus extra for greasing
125 g/4 oz demerara sugar
2 tbsp golden syrup
175 g/6 oz jumbo porridge oats
few drops vanilla extract

Preheat the oven to 160°C/325°F/Gas Mark 3. Butter a
20.5 cm/8 inch square baking tin.

Place the butter or margarine, sugar and golden syrup in a
saucepan and heat gently until the butter has melted and
every grain of sugar has dissolved.

Remove from the heat and stir in the oats and vanilla extract.
Stir well and then spoon the mixture into the prepared tin.

Smooth level with the back of a large spoon. Bake in the
centre of the oven for 30–40 minutes until golden. Leave to
cool in the tin for 10 minutes, then mark into fingers and
leave in the tin until completely cold. When cold, cut into
fingers with a sharp knife.

Store in an airtight tin for up to 1 week.

Lemon Drizzle Cake

Cuts into 9

125 g/4 oz butter or margarine
175 g/6 oz caster sugar
2 large eggs
175 g/6 oz self-raising flour
2 lemons, preferably unwaxed
50 g/2 oz granulated sugar

Preheat the oven to 180°C/350°F/Gas Mark 4, 10 minutes before baking. Lightly oil and line the base of an 18 cm/7 inch square cake tin with baking paper. In a large bowl, cream the butter or margarine and sugar together until soft and fluffy.

Beat the eggs, then gradually add a little of the egg to the creamed mixture, adding 1 tablespoon of flour after each addition.

Finely grate the zest from 1 of the lemons and stir into the creamed mixture, beating well until smooth. Squeeze the juice from the lemon, strain, and then stir into the mixture. Spoon into the prepared tin, level the surface and bake in the preheated oven for 25–30 minutes.

Using a zester, remove the peel from the last lemon and mix with 25 g/1 oz of the granulated sugar and reserve. Squeeze the juice into a small saucepan. Add the rest of the granulated sugar to the lemon juice in the saucepan and heat gently, stirring occasionally. When the sugar has dissolved, simmer gently for 3–4 minutes until syrupy.

With a cocktail stick or fine skewer prick the cake all over. Sprinkle the lemon zest and sugar syrup over the top of the cake, drizzle over the syrup and leave to cool in the tin. Cut the cake into squares and serve.

Store for 1 week in an airtight tin.

Carrot Cake

Cuts into 8–10

200 g/7 oz plain flour
$^1/_2$ tsp ground cinnamon
1$^1/_2$ tsp freshly grated nutmeg
1 tsp baking powder
1 tsp bicarbonate of soda
150 g/5 oz dark muscovado sugar
200 ml/7 fl oz vegetable or sunflower oil
3 medium eggs
225 g/8 oz carrots, peeled and roughly grated
50 g/2 oz chopped walnuts

For the icing:

175 g/6 oz cream cheese
finely grated zest of 1 orange
1 tbsp orange juice
1 tsp vanilla extract
125 g/4 oz icing sugar

Preheat the oven to 150°C/300°F/Gas Mark 2, 10 minutes before baking. Lightly oil and line the base of a 15 cm/6 inch deep square cake tin with greaseproof paper or baking parchment.

Sift the flour, spices, baking powder and bicarbonate of soda together into a large bowl. Stir in the dark muscovado sugar and mix together.

Lightly whisk the oil and eggs together, then gradually stir into the flour and sugar mixture. Stir well. Add the carrots and walnuts. Mix thoroughly and then pour into the prepared cake tin. Bake in the preheated oven for 1$^1/_4$ hours, or until light and springy to the touch and a skewer inserted into the centre of the cake comes out clean. Remove from the oven and allow to cool in the tin then turn out onto a wire rack. Leave until cold.

To make the icing, beat together the cream cheese, orange zest, orange juice and vanilla extract. Sift the icing sugar and stir into the cream cheese mixture.

When cold, discard the lining paper, spread the cream cheese icing over the top and serve cut into squares.

Store for 4–5 days, lightly covered in the refrigerator. I would not recommend freezing.

Easy Victoria Sponge

Cuts into 8–10

225 g/8 oz softened butter
or margarine
225 g/8 oz caster sugar
4 medium eggs
1 tsp vanilla extract
225 g/8 oz self-raising flour
1 tsp baking powder
icing sugar, to dust

For the filling:

4 tbsp seedless
raspberry jam
100 ml/3^1/$_2$ fl oz whipping cream
(optional)

Preheat the oven to 180°C/350°F/Gas Mark 4. Grease two 20.5 cm/8 inch sandwich tins and line the bases with nonstick baking parchment.

Place the butter or margarine, sugar, eggs and vanilla extract in a large bowl and sift in the flour and baking powder. Beat for about 2 minutes until smooth and blended, then divide between the tins and smooth level.

Bake for about 25 minutes until golden, well risen and the tops of the cakes spring back when lightly touched with a fingertip. Leave to cool in the tins for at least 5 minutes, then turn out onto a wire rack to cool. When cold, peel away the baking parchment.

When completely cold, spread one cake with jam and place on a serving plate. Whip the cream, if using, until it forms soft peaks, then spread on the underside of the other cake. Sandwich the two cakes together and sift a little icing sugar over the top.

Keep lightly covered in the refrigerator for 4–5 days.

If liked, the cake can be frozen in portions. Cut into portions and place on a plate. Freeze without wrapping, then, once solid, wrap in freezer wrap or kitchen foil. Label and date. Use within 2 weeks. When wishing to thaw, take out of the freezer and leave for 3–4 hours until soft.

Raspberry Butterfly Cupcakes

Makes 6–7

50 g/2 oz caster sugar
50 g/2 oz softened butter
or margarine
1 medium egg
50 g/2 oz self-raising flour
1/4 tsp baking powder
1/2 tsp vanilla extract

To decorate:

2 tbsp seedless raspberry jam
6–7 fresh raspberries
icing sugar, to dust

Preheat the oven to 190°C/375°F/Gas Mark 5. Line a bun trays with 6–7 paper cases, depending on the depth of the holes.

Place all the cupcake ingredients in a large bowl and beat with an electric mixer or wooden spoon for about 2 minutes until smooth. Fill the paper cases halfway up with the mixture.

Bake for about 15 minutes until firm, risen and golden. Remove to a wire rack to cool. When cold, cut a small circle out of the top of each cupcake and then cut the circle in half to form wings.

Fill each cupcake with a teaspoon of raspberry jam. Replace the wings at an angle and top each with a fresh raspberry. Dust lightly with icing sugar and serve immediately.

If wishing to store, omit the fresh raspberries. Keep for up to 1 week in an airtight tin. It is not necessary to freeze.

Chocolate ❧ Fruit Crumble

Makes 4 portions

For the crumble:

125 g/4 oz plain flour
125 g/4 oz softened butter
or margarine
75 g/3 oz light soft brown sugar
50 g/2 oz rolled porridge oats
50 g/2 oz hazelnuts, chopped

For the filling:

450 g/1 lb Bramley apples
1 tbsp lemon juice
50 g/2 oz sultanas
50 g/2 oz seedless raisins
50 g/2 oz light soft brown sugar
350 g/12 oz pears, peeled, cored
and chopped
1 tsp ground cinnamon
125 g/4 oz dark chocolate, very
roughly chopped
2 tsp caster sugar for sprinkling

Preheat the oven to 190°C/375°F/Gas Mark 5, 10 minutes before baking. Lightly oil an ovenproof dish. For the crumble, sift the flour into a large bowl. Cut the butter or margarine into small dice and add to the flour. Rub the butter or margarine into the flour until the mixture resembles fine breadcrumbs. Stir the sugar, porridge oats and chopped hazelnuts into the mixture and reserve.

For the filling, peel the apples, core and slice thickly. Place in a large heavy-based saucepan with the lemon juice and 3 tablespoons water. Add the sultanas, raisins and soft brown sugar. Bring slowly to the boil, cover and simmer over a gentle heat for 8–10 minutes, stirring occasionally, until the apples are slightly softened. Remove the saucepan from the heat and leave to cool slightly before stirring in the pears, ground cinnamon and the chopped chocolate. Spoon into the prepared ovenproof dish. Sprinkle the crumble evenly over the top then bake in the preheated oven for 35–40 minutes until the top is golden. Remove from the oven, sprinkle with the caster sugar and serve immediately.

Any remaining crumble can be spooned into a clean dish and covered with clingfilm. Keep overnight in the refrigerator. Do not freeze. The crumble will reheat well in the microwave. Pierce the clingfilm 2–3 times then heat on High for 2 minutes. Allow to stand for 1 minute then serve.

Chocolate Mousse with Raisins

Makes 4 portions

200 g/7 oz dark chocolate
150 ml/¼ pint ready-made custard
300 ml/½ pint whipping cream
1 tbsp strong black coffee
125 g/4 oz raisins
1 medium egg white
chocolate curls, to decorate

Break the chocolate into small pieces and place in a small heatproof bowl set over a saucepan of gently simmering water. Heat gently, stirring occasionally, until the chocolate has melted and is smooth. Remove the bowl from the heat and leave to stand for about 10 minutes, or until the chocolate cools and begins to thicken. Using a metal spoon or rubber spatula, carefully fold in the prepared custard.

Whip the cream until soft peaks form, reserve a little for decorating and fold the rest into the chocolate custard mixture together with the coffee. Gently stir in the raisins.

Whisk the egg white in a clean, grease-free bowl, until stiff but not dry, then fold 1 tablespoon into the chocolate mixture and mix together lightly. Add the remaining egg white and stir lightly until well mixed. Spoon into 4 tall glasses and chill in the refrigerator for up to 2 hours.

Just before serving, top with whipped cream and decorate with the chocolate curls, then serve.

Keep any uneaten mousse in the refrigerator for up to 2 days. Do not freeze.

Chocolate Pancakes

Makes 2 portions

For the pancakes:
40 g/1¹/2 oz plain flour
2 tsp cocoa powder
1 tsp caster sugar
2 medium eggs
85 ml/3 fl oz milk
40 g/1¹/2 oz unsalted butter, melted

For the mango sauce:
200 g/7 oz canned mango
or 1 small ripe mango,
peeled and diced
50 ml/2 fl oz clear apple
juice or white wine
1 tbsp, or to taste, golden
caster sugar

For the filling:
125 g/4 oz dark chocolate
50 ml/2 fl oz whipping cream
2 small eggs, separated
15 g/¹/2 oz golden caster sugar

Preheat the oven to 200°C/400°F/Gas Mark 6, 15 minutes before cooking. Sift the flour, cocoa powder and sugar into a bowl and make a well in the centre. Beat the eggs and milk together, then beat into the flour mixture. Stir in 15 g/¹/2 oz of the melted butter and leave to stand for 1 hour. Heat an 18 cm/7 inch frying pan and brush with melted butter. Add about 3 tbsp of the batter and swirl to cover the base of the pan. Cook over a medium heat for 1–2 minutes, flip over and cook for a further 40 seconds. Repeat with the remaining batter. Stack the pancakes, interleaving with greaseproof paper.

To make the sauce, place the mango, apple juice or white wine and sugar in a pan. Bring to the boil over a medium heat, then simmer for 2–3 minutes, stirring constantly. When it has thickened, chill in the refrigerator.

For the filling, melt the chocolate and cream in a pan over a medium heat. Stir until smooth, then cool. Beat the yolks with the caster sugar for 3–5 minutes until the mixture is pale and creamy, then beat in the chocolate mixture. Whisk the egg whites until stiff, and add a little to the mixture. Stir in the remainder. Spoon a little of the mixture onto a pancake. Fold in half, then in half again. Repeat with the rest. Brush with butter and bake for 15–20 minutes until the filling is set. Serve hot or cold with the mango sauce.

The pancakes can be refrigerated for up to 2 days, wrapped in clingfilm with the paper separating them, or frozen in a freezer bag for up to 2 weeks. If frozen, allow to thaw overnight. Reheat by frying in a lightly oiled pan.

Fruited French Toast

Makes 1–2 portions

2 slices spicy fruit loaf,
about 1 cm/^{1}/$_2$ inch thick
50 ml/2 fl oz milk
2 tbsp orange juice
1 medium egg yolk
^{1}/$_4$ tsp, or to taste, ground cinnamon
15 g/^{1}/$_2$ oz unsalted butter
1 tbsp sunflower oil
2–3 tbsp seedless
raspberry jam or conserve

For the orange cream:

125 ml/4 fl oz whipping cream
1 tsp icing sugar
1 tbsp finely grated orange zest
2 tsp orange juice

Cut the crusts off the bread, and then cut each slice diagonally into four triangles. Mix together half the milk and 1 tablespoon of the orange juice. Quickly dip the bread triangles in the mixture, and then place on a wire rack over a tray to drain.

Beat together the egg yolk, cinnamon, remaining milk and any milk on the tray. Dip the triangles in the egg and return to the rack.

Heat half the butter and the oil in a frying pan or wok. Add the bread triangles about three at a time and fry on both sides until well browned. Remove and keep warm in a low oven, while cooking the rest. When needed, add the remaining butter and finish cooking the bread triangles. Add to those keeping warm in the oven while making the sauce.

Gently heat the jam in a small saucepan with the remaining 1 tablespoon of orange juice and 1 tablespoon water until melted, and then cook for 1 minute.

To make the orange cream, whisk the cream, icing sugar, orange zest and orange juice together until soft peaks form. Serve the French toasts drizzled with the jam sauce and accompanied by the orange cream. These toasts will not keep, so it's a good excuse to invite a friend round to share.

Index

A
Aduki Bean & Rice Burgers 176

B
Baby Onion Risotto 174
Bacon & Split Pea Soup 78
Baked Macaroni Cheese 114
beans
    Aduki Bean & Rice Burgers 176
    Black Bean Chilli with Avocado
        Salsa 188
    Cassoulet 202
    Italian Bean Soup 74
beef
    Chilli Con Carne with Crispy-skinned
        Potato 182
    Lasagne 130
    Spaghetti Bolognese 128
Black Bean Chilli with Avocado
    Salsa 188
Braised Chicken in Beer 206
Bread & Tomato Soup 80
Bulgur Wheat Salad with Minty Lemon
    Dressing 108

C
cake
    Carrot Cake 240
    Easy Victoria Sponge 242

Lemon Drizzle Cake 238
    Raspberry Butterfly Cupcakes 244
    Chocolate Fudge Brownies 234
Caribbean-style Chicken Stew 158
Carrot & Ginger Soup 68
Carrot Cake 240
Cassoulet 202
Chargrilled Vegetable & Goats' Cheese
    Pizza 190
cheese
    Baked Macaroni Cheese 114
    Chargrilled Vegetable & Goats'
        Cheese Pizza 190
    Cheesy Chicken Burgers 208
    Paneer & Pea Curry 162
    Potato Skins 86
Cheesy Chicken Burgers 208
chicken see poultry
Chicken & Lentil Curry 144
Chicken & Summer Vegetable
    Risotto 224
Chicken Pie with Sweet Potato
    Topping 204
Chicken with Mushrooms &
    Cream 216
Chicken with Noodles 138
Chicken Wraps 96
Chilli Con Carne with Crispy-skinned
    Potato 182

Chinese Chicken Soup 82
Chinese Fried Rice 88
Chocolate & Fruit Crumble 246
Chocolate Chip Cookies 232
Chocolate Fudge Brownies 234
Chocolate Mousse with Raisins 248
Chocolate Pancakes 250
Classic Flapjacks 236
Classic Minestrone 212
Creamy Turkey & Tomato Pasta 214
Curried Parsnip Soup 66
Curried Potatoes with Spinach 152

E
Easy Victoria Sponge 242
Egg & Aubergine Curry 164
Egg & Bacon Pie 198

F
fish
    Malaysian Fish Curry 154
    Mediterranean Feast 90
    Smoked Haddock Rösti 98
    Spanish Omelette with Fish 94
    Tuna & Mushroom Ragout 196
Fruited French Toast 252
Fusilli Pasta with Spicy Tomato
    Salsa 124

G
Garlic Mushroom Galettes 104
Gnocchetti with Broccoli & Bacon
      Sauce 118

H
Huevos Rancheros 102

I
Italian Bean Soup 74

K
Kerala Pork Curry 150

L
lamb
   Lamb Balti 156
   Shepherd's Pie 200
Lamb Balti 156
Lasagne 130
Leek & Ham Risotto 218
Lemon Chicken with Potatoes,
      Rosemary & Olives 222
Lemon Drizzle Cake 238
lentils
   Chicken & Lentil Curry 144
   Spinach Dhal 146
   Vegetable & Lentil Casserole 192

M
Malaysian Fish Curry 154
Mediterranean Feast 90
mushrooms
   Chicken with Mushrooms & Cream 216
   Garlic Mushroom Galettes 104

Tuna & Mushroom Ragout 196
Turkey & Mushroom Lasagne 122

N
noodles
   Chicken with Noodles 138
   Chinese Chicken Soup 82
   Pork Fried Noodles 136
   Turkey Chow Mein 140
   Warm Noodle Salad 134

P
Paneer & Pea Curry 162
pasta
   Baked Macaroni Cheese 114
   Classic Minestrone 212
   Creamy Turkey & Tomato Pasta 214
   Fusilli Pasta with Spicy Tomato
      Salsa 124
   Gnocchetti with Broccoli & Bacon
      Sauce 118
   Italian Bean Soup 74
   Lasagne 130
   Penne with Mixed Peppers &
      Garlic 116
   Sausage & Redcurrant Pasta
      Bake 132
   Spaghetti Bolognese 128
   Spaghetti with Turkey & Bacon
      Sauce 126
   Turkey & Mushroom Lasagne 122
   Vegetarian Spaghetti Bolognese 120
Penne with Mixed Peppers & Garlic 116
pork
   Bacon & Split Pea Soup 78

Cassoulet 202
Egg & Bacon Pie 198
Kerala Pork Curry 150
Leek & Ham Risotto 218
Pork Chop Hotpot 226
Pork Fried Noodles 136
Pork Sausages with Onion Gravy &
      Best-ever Mash 186
Sausage & Bacon Risotto 178
Sausage & Redcurrant Pasta
      Bake 132
Sweet & Sour Pork 166
Toad in the Hole 228
Pork Chop Hotpot 226
Pork Fried Noodles 136
Pork Sausages with Onion Gravy &
      Best-ever Mash 186
potato
   Chargrilled Vegetable & Goats'
      Cheese Pizza 190
   Chicken Pie with Sweet Potato
      Topping 204
   Chilli Con Carne with Crispy-skinned
      Potato 182
   Curried Potatoes with Spinach 152
   Lemon Chicken with Potatoes,
      Rosemary & Olives 222
   Pork Sausages with Onion Gravy &
      Best-ever Mash 186
   Potato Skins 86
   Potatoes, Leek & Rosemary Soup 72
   Shepherd's Pie 200
   Slow Roast Chicken with Potatoes &
      Oregano 220
   Smoked Haddock Rösti 98

Spanish Omelette with Fish 94
Swede, Turnip, Parsnip & Potato
    Soup 70
Thai-style Cauliflower & Potato
    Curry 160
Turkey Hash with Potato &
    Beetroot 100
Potato Skins 86
Potatoes, Leek & Rosemary Soup 72
poultry
    Braised Chicken in Beer 206
    Caribbean-style Chicken Stew 158
    Cheesy Chicken Burgers 208
    Chicken & Lentil Curry 144
    Chicken & Summer Vegetable
        Risotto 224
    Chicken Pie with Sweet Potato
        Topping 204
    Chicken with Mushrooms & Cream 216
    Chicken with Noodles 138
    Chicken Wraps 96
    Chinese Chicken Soup 82
    Creamy Turkey & Tomato Pasta 214
    Lemon Chicken with Potatoes,
        Rosemary & Olives 222
    Slow Roast Chicken with Potatoes &
        Oregano 220
    Spaghetti with Turkey & Bacon
        Sauce 126
    Thai Coconut Chicken 170
    Thai Green Chicken Curry 148
    Turkey & Mushroom Lasagne 122
    Turkey Chow Mein 140
    Turkey Hash with Potato &
        Beetroot 100
Pumpkin Soup 64

R
Raspberry Butterfly Cupcakes 244
Ratatouille 184
rice
    Aduki Bean & Rice Burgers 176
    Baby Onion Risotto 174
    Chicken & Summer Vegetable
        Risotto 224
    Chinese Fried Rice 88
    Leek & Ham Risotto 218
    Rice & Tomato Soup 76
    Rice Nuggets in Herby Tomato
        Sauce 168
    Rice-filled Peppers 172
    Sausage & Bacon Risotto 178
    Spanish Baked Tomatoes 106
    Thai Coconut Chicken 170
Rice & Tomato Soup 76
Rice Nuggets in Herby Tomato
    Sauce 168
Rice-filled Peppers 172
Roasted Butternut Squash 194
Roasted Mixed Vegetables with Garlic
    & Herb Sauce 110

S
Sausage & Bacon Risotto 178
Sausage & Redcurrant Pasta Bake 132
Shepherd's Pie 200
Slow Roast Chicken with Potatoes &
    Oregano 220
soup
    Bacon & Split Pea Soup 78
    Bread & Tomato Soup 80
    Carrot & Ginger Soup 68
    Chinese Chicken Soup 82
    Curried Parsnip Soup 66

    Italian Bean Soup 74
    Potatoes, Leek & Rosemary Soup 72
    Pumpkin Soup 64
    Rice & Tomato Soup 76
    Swede, Turnip, Parsnip & Potato
        Soup 70
Smoked Haddock Rösti 98
Spaghetti Bolognese 128
Spaghetti with Turkey & Bacon
        Sauce 126
Spanish Baked Tomatoes 106
Spanish Omelette with Fish 94
Spinach Dhal 146
Swede, Turnip, Parsnip & Potato
        Soup 70
Sweet & Sour Pork 166
Sweetcorn Fritters 92

T
Thai Coconut Chicken 170
Thai Green Chicken Curry 148
Thai-style Cauliflower & Potato Curry 160

Toad in the Hole 228
Tuna & Mushroom Ragout 196
Turkey & Mushroom Lasagne 122
Turkey Chow Mein 140
Turkey Hash with Potato & Beetroot 100

V
Vegetable & Lentil Casserole 192
Vegetarian Spaghetti Bolognese 120

W
Warm Noodle Salad 134
Winter Hotchpot 84